William Leonard Gage

Helen on her travels

What she saw and what she did in Europe

William Leonard Gage

Helen on her travels
What she saw and what she did in Europe

ISBN/EAN: 9783337210847

Printed in Europe, USA, Canada, Australia, Japan

Cover: Foto ©Andreas Hilbeck / pixelio.de

More available books at **www.hansebooks.com**

HELEN ON HER TRAVELS:

WHAT SHE SAW AND WHAT SHE DID

IN

EUROPE.

NEW YORK:
PUBLISHED BY HURD & HOUGHTON,
459 BROOME STREET.
1868.

HELEN ON HER TRAVELS.

FIRST LETTER.

EDINBURGH.

DEAR LITTLE COUSIN SUSIE:

I am very much afraid that this will not be a very good letter, but I have wanted to see you so much, and tell you what nice things there are in Europe, that mamma says I may try to write a real letter to you, as that will be the next best thing to seeing you.

Oh, I do miss you so much! When I am playing with my dolls, I feel lonely without you. There are some very nice little girls here, though, but they are not my cousins, you know! But I shall forget what I want to tell you about, and I think you would like to hear about my ride on the ocean, and it was a very long ride, Susie, I thought.

When we went one night from Boston to New York in one of the Sound boats, as papa called it, I thought it was the most delightful thing to ride on a steamboat. It was so large, and the great saloons had such beautiful carpets and sofas, and the people looked so happy, and I had such a pretty bed to sleep in, that I wished we would not get to New York so soon, and I told mamma we should have such a nice time all the way to Europe, because we went in a steamboat.

But oh dear, Susie! it was very different from what I thought. We did not have such a beautiful great state-room to sleep in, and the ship did not sail so nicely through the water, but very soon began to roll so much that people could hardly walk about. And then on the deck, the children could not be trusted to run and play for fear of falling into the ocean. And at the table, too, the dishes could n't be trusted to keep in their places, but were held in a kind of frame, so they would n't fall into our laps.

But I had a nice time after all, for there were a good many little children to play with, and one little girl like me had four sisters and two brothers. Was n't that nice? We used to have our tea sets and dolls and books, and then every day we went up on deck to walk and jump. I was not allowed to sit at the same table with papa and mamma, when they had their meals, but we children had a table by ourselves in another room, and had the stewardess to wait upon us. When we were good she would give us nice things to eat; but one little boy was naughty once, and she sent him away without any pudding. We did n't have nuts and apples at our table, but there was one nice gentlemen from Cuba who was so kind to us, and he would throw a whole handful of nuts and figs on the floor for us to run and pick up.

The captain liked little children, too, and he told a sailor to make a nice swing for us on deck, but before we could have any good time with it, a great storm came and we had to stay with our mothers. I remember one day when I was at your house it rained all day, but we could run about in the house and play, and aunt Susan, that is your grandma, told us nice stories, so that it was almost better than a pleasant day. Grandmas tell such nice stories; do n't you think they do, Susie?

But in that great storm when we were on the Atlantic ocean, it wasn't much like that. The great rooms were all dark, because they thought the waves would break in the windows overhead, if they were not covered with boards. We could n't have much to eat, for everything would roll off the tables, and there were such awful noises all the time, things rolling about, dishes breaking, people falling down, and the great waves thumping against the ship all the time.

The captain said we must all be good children, and he hoped God would n't let us be drowned. So we kept still, and we could n't have done any thing else, it was so dreadful. We could just see around the room by a little light from the lamps, and I thought people's faces looked very pale. And I was afraid, too, when papa put me into my bed, and placed a high board before it, so I could not fall out. It seemed just like lying in a deep box. I said, "Now I lay me," to papa, and he prayed a little prayer too, and I cried; I couldn't help it, and I thought he did, too, though he tried to look cheerful.

But when I woke up the next morning the weather was not so bad, and in a few days more, we could see Ireland, and then England, and then we stopped at Liverpool, a great city in England.

Have you liked this letter, Susie? Then I'll write another, perhaps.

Second Letter.

EDINBURGH.

Dear Susie:

Mamma asked me this morning, if it was not time to write to you again. I know it is, but I think it is rather hard to write a whole letter, do n't you? And then every body forgets so much they would like to say, certainly I do. Now, in that first letter to you, I meant to have told you what we did when Sabbath day came, when we were on that great steamer. They were not much like home Sundays, for we had no Sunday school, and I like to go to Sunday school. How I did long to see my teacher and the little boys and girls in my class! But we had a meeting: we went to church in our cabin, and the minister was dressed in a black silk gown, and had white bands around his neck. He read all the prayers, and some from the bible, and then, when all the people read, we children read too. He preached a long sermon, but we all kept still, and all the steerage passengers came who wished to, and they listened to all he said. I liked our meeting very much, but the rest of the day seemed so long. Now, Susie, you see I forgot to tell you all this in the other letter.

Oh, how glad I was when papa said we were going to go on to the land again; but I kept close to papa for there were so many people crowding and shouting. We had no friends to meet us, but some of the passengers had, and it almost made us cry so see them so happy. One lady stood on the shore, and when she saw her daughter on the little boat, for the great ship can't sail close to the land, she said, "My child, my child; thank God for my child again."

The first thing we did when we stepped off the boat was to go into a great depot, to see some men look over our baggage. Papa said it was the law that if we carried anything in our trunks to England that wasn't allowed, we should have to pay money. I was afraid they would hurt my doll if they found her, for I carried my great one called Rosa, but the men did n't disturb our things much, for they seemed to feel we had no things hid. That gentleman from Cuba who gave us so many nuts on the ship, had given mamma a bunch of little cigars, such as the ladies in Cuba smoke, but she did n't have to pay for them; but we heard of one man who had to give up a great many cigars because he tried to hide them.

When the trunks were locked again, papa sent them to the depot where we were going to take the cars for Scotland, and then we had a little time to walk about. I saw so many great ships, they seemed to come right up to the streets, but papa said they were in the great docks; that means very deep places filled with water. And oh, there were all kinds of carriages so different from ours, and the ones people rode in they called cabs, but they did n't look so nice as the Boston coaches, I thought. I always thought when I walked down Washington street, in Boston, that there were as many people as in London, but I found a great many more in Liverpool. The houses were so high, and the bricks so dark, and there was so much smoke, and oh, how many great churches we saw, and we went into a great hall, so great that it took me some time to run across it; and then we walked through beautiful squares, and saw many fine houses, and nice looking people and such pretty stores; oh, I forget, they call them shops in England; and the bread stores were the most tempting I ever saw, and I had some nice buns to eat. But they did n't have any of Brown's troches there, for we could n't find anything for my cough but some liquorice lozenges. But the place I liked to see the best was the market. We all laughed to see the women bareheaded standing out of doors selling hens and meat and cabbages and flowers and all kinds of things. One woman had a barrel of potatoes tipped over, and some little boys were running away with them. And there were so many people buying, and so many people selling, that there was a great noise and a great crowding, and we had to walk in the middle of the street. I saw some pretty baskets, and mamma said one would be so convenient for a luncheon basket that we bought one. I wanted to get a little one for you, but then I thought I could not carry it over Europe, very well. I want to see you, Susie, so much, and two other little girls I know, Mary and Anna, that I almost want to go back to America.

But I have written all I can to-day. We only after that went to the depot. No, first we had our dinner, and then we waited till the cars started. If mamma will allow me to write again, I will tell you what strange cars they have in England.

I send you a good bye kiss, and Aunt Susan, too.

THIRD LETTER.

EDINBURGH.

DEAR COUSIN SUSIE:

What did I say I would write about this time? Was it about the cars I rode in to Scotland? You never saw such a great depot as that one we started from in Liverpool, and you would hardly have known at first where to find the ladies' room. But pretty soon mamma and I found two, and each was marked with a different sign; one was "first class waiting room," and the other "second and third class." We looked into both and they were very different from each other, for one had nice tables and sofas and chairs and looking-glasses, and was so nicely warmed, too, and no one seemed to dare to go in but very nicely dressed ladies; but the other was very cheerless and rather cold and untidy. But papa called us to get into the cars, though I thought he must be mistaken about there being any ready, for I had heard no whistle, and all was so quiet.

As we walked along on the platform, two or three men rushed up to us; one wanted to take mamma's travelling bag, and one papa's umbrella, and another looked at me in such a way that I was afraid he thought me a kind of bundle, and would catch me up, too. It seemed very polite, though, for them to be so kind, didn't it, Susie? But, bye and bye, I saw papa had to give every man some money who had done anything for us, and I thought it was better to do as people in America do, to wait upon themselves. But the cars were ready for us; still the people seemed in no hurry, and men dressed in a kind of uniform stood here and there beside the train, to prevent anybody from pushing and crowding, and to see that everybody found a seat.

The cars,—but we mustn't call them cars, Susie, but carriages; isn't it strange?—had doors on each side instead of at the ends, and each carriage was divided into three or four little rooms, as I called them, with the seats facing each other. Six or eight people could ride in each one. The outside of all the doors were numbered either "first class," "second class," or "third class." We had time to look into all, and the first class ones were much the best. The seats were stuffed and covered with plush, and they were divided from each other so nicely, that each one was like a comfortable arm chair. The little curtains at the windows were so pretty, and it seemed like being in a pleasant little room. But the second class cars were not so nice, for they had only plain wooden seats, and no curtains at all to the windows. The third class ones were not much different, only there were not such divisions made, but all the people in the car could see each other, just as we can in America, only the seats were arranged so differently. And, Susie, which one would you like best to ride in? I know what you will say; but it costs much more money to ride in the prettiest ones than in the others.

But I am tired writing so much about one thing. Oh, I was glad to ride on a railroad again, and to think I was going to Scotland! I did n't know exactly where Scotland was, but I wanted to go. First, we had to go through a very long, black tunnel, but after that we had such a nice time! The sun was shining, and it was so warm that we could have one window open, and I stood a long time looking out. At first I did n't like the motion of the cars very well, for we seemed to shake from side to side; but I could n't think of that long, for there were so many pretty things to see. The houses were all of brick, and each one had a little garden in front, full of flowers, and sometimes vegetables. We saw a great many villages, and each one had such an odd looking little church; and we saw some great cities, but they did n't seem so pretty. And when we were going through the country, with no houses near us, the banks near the railroad were covered with grass, so there was no dust.

Whenever the train stopped, the guards opened the doors, and saw that people had time enough to get out. I was very glad when one of our companions stopped, and then we had the little room all to ourselves. Mamma gave me something good from her luncheon basket, and said, after I had seen the beautiful sunset, I might lie down. She said we were in the lake region then. I don't remember anything after that, till we changed cars and had some supper. Then in the new cars, I think I must have gone to sleep, for the first I knew papa was saying to me, "Wake up, Helen, we have got to Edinburgh!"

Do I write too long letters, Susie?

FOURTH LETTER.

EDINBURGH.

DEAR COUSIN SUSIE:

I am going to take a long walk this morning, but mamma says that I must first go on with my story to you. Oh, I wish you were here, and then you could see all that I do, and it would be so much pleasanter than writing and reading a letter, would n't it?

When I woke up the first morning we were here, I thought of course I was in my little berth in the steamer, and began to wonder why I was not rocking back and forth. It was so still I looked around, and saw a very different room from my little state-room, it was so large, and had such great beds and windows. I was so happy that I sprang up and was partly dressed before mamma woke up. When we were all ready we went down stairs into a beautiful room to get our breakfast, and we had a little table to ourselves. It stood by a great bow window, and all the time we were eating I kept jumping up and looking out, for there was such a fine prospect before us. It seems as though we must be in another world, too, all looked so unlike Boston and any place in America that I ever saw. Don't you want to know what we had for breakfast, Susie? It was only bread and butter and coffee; but bread and butter never tasted so good before, and then I had some coffee in a pretty china cup, and a little silver sugar bowl and milk pitcher for my own use. I am not allowed very often to have coffee to drink, so this was a treat.

Just before I had finished eating, two ladies came in with a dear little girl; she was just the size of my dear little friend Annie, at home, and mamma gave me permission to speak to her. I could hardly understand what she said, for she spoke as the Scotch people do; but I couldn't help loving her dearly, she was so gentle. While papa and mamma were reading the morning papers, we stood together at the window, and we could look right down upon the street,— Princes Street, it is called,— and there were a great many little children going to school, and just on the other side was a great monument, and behind that were the most beautiful gardens I ever saw, full of pretty walks and green grass and flowers.

But I can't remember nearly all I saw and did that day, nor the next, until we came here to our friends, so I will skip that, Susie, and tell you now what a nice house I am in, and who lives here. Oh, we do have such nice times; that means Jessie and Maggie and me. And Jackie, too; I forgot Jackie, just then. He is, next to my little friend Walter at home, almost the dearest little boy I ever saw; he dresses just like a Highlander, with a black velvet frock and short trousers and red stockings, and such a pretty plaid sash tied over his shoulder. He is never naughty, but is just as polite as a gentleman. And they all have such pretty playthings, which we play with up stairs in the nursery; and Jessie and Maggie have each a little bed up there, too, and I sleep with Maggie. She is two years older than I am, and she is so roguish, and such a nice girl to play with, and Jessie is older than Maggie, and she is more quiet, but I love her just as much.

Every morning we get up early, and Margaret helps us dress; then we go to the school-room, a little room down stairs, where the governess comes, and where the school-books are, and eat our porridge and milk. Jessie's mamma and my mamma come and bid us good morning, and then we go together to the dining room, where we have family prayers. Then when the family have their breakfast, we are allowed some bread and butter. While the governess is giving Jessie and Maggie their music and other lessons, Jackie and I play, or go to walk with Margaret. We don't have our dinner with the others, but eat earlier in the nice little school-room; only when our mammas eat we have some of the dessert; and sometimes when they have tea we get a little piece of cake, too. I think the Scotch children don't eat so many rich things as the American children do, for I never hear even little

Jackie beg for any. This is such a beautiful house: great rooms, and halls, and pictures, and so many nice things,— and this afternoon Maggie and I are going to dress up her doll with —

But mamma calls me to go to walk, so good bye, dear cousin Susie.

Fifth Letter.
EDINBURGH.

Dear Susie:

Jessie and Maggie are studying in the school-room, and Jackie has gone to walk, but I have such a bad cold that I am not allowed to go out, so I think I will surprise mamma by having another letter ready for you. I hardly know what to write about, this time, unless I tell you about Sabbath day, that was day before yesterday.

Anybody would have known it was Sunday, because after breakfast and prayers we did n't have our playthings about, but we had nice books to read. I never saw so many pretty books! There were so many Bible stories, with beautiful pictures, that I had n't time enough to see them all before mamma called me to get ready for church. The churches do n't look like ours at home, Susie; they are very large, and the pews are not so comfortable, and the minister stands in such a high pulpit; and just above his head is a kind of cover or framework of wood, which Jessie told me was called a sounding board. After church I heard papa say there used to be some in America, a good many years ago. It was built out from the wall, and it seemed to me all the time as though it would fall.

When the minister came in he looked some like the minister on the ocean, for he had on a black gown and white bands, and one man walked before him and carried the Bible and opened the pulpit door for him, then he went away; and another gentleman walked behind him, and he stopped just under the high pulpit, where there was a little desk. He was the one who read the hymns to the people, and commenced their singing for them. There wasn't any organ at all, but this gentleman read two lines, and then all the people sung them together, and then two more, and so on, through it all. Everybody sung as though they liked it, but they sung very slowly. I mean the tunes were so slow. You know, Susie, that I never sat so still in church as you did, but I tried very hard this time, for if I moved it seemed as though everybody was looking right at me. All the little children I saw were just as quiet as their fathers and mothers. I liked the minister very much, because he was Maggie's grandpa.

I didn't have any money to put into the plate at the door, because I didn't know about it; and when I saw the others drop in a penny apiece, I was so sorry I hadn't carried mine. Everybody lays a piece of money on the great plate when they go into church, and I think the children give a penny.

I almost wished the meeting would be over, so I could go with Maggie to Sunday school; but there wasn't any, Susie! We went right home from church; but we did have a kind of Sunday school at home, for we learned Bible verses, and Margaret told us good stories, and we all sung pretty hymns, and then grandma talked to us, too. Oh, Jessie's grandma is the dearest lady! No, Susie, not dearer than your grandma, but we all loved her dearly. She never allows the children to be naughty, and Jessie and Maggie and Jackie never are naughty; all the time I have been here they have never spoken unkindly to each other.

When bed-time came I thought I never had had a happier Sunday, only it was such a disappointment about the Sunday school. But now, Susie, I've got something funny to tell you about the Sunday school, for there is one, after all, only it is in the evening, and poor children generally go, and those who do not get much good said to them at home. And Sunday evening my papa went there with Jessie's papa, because he is a teacher there, Jessie's papa is, and after the lessons were through my papa talked to them a little, and he told them he lived in America, and I suppose about the Sunday schools there. When papa was going out he heard one little boy whisper to another, "A North American Indian!" Just as though he thought all the people in America must be Indians. I am sure papa doesn't look much like an Indian, does he, Susie?

SIXTH LETTER.

EDINBURGH.

DEAR COUSIN SUSIE:

I am so afraid I shall forget to tell you all I mean to in this letter. We have had a very nice time this week, and Edinburgh is the finest city I ever saw, and has the prettiest walks. The streets are very broad and clean, and the houses are built of such nice looking stone, and are so regular, and there are so many large squares with a great monument in the centre and green grass all around, and the shop windows are so full of pretty things, that it makes me feel as though I would like to be a little Scotch girl, too. You never saw in your whole life, Susie, as many bread shops as I see every time I go out; and they are so clean, and have all kinds of cake in them, beside bread. I like the Scotch short-cake very much, though mamma says it is too rich for children to eat. They do n't have the shops arranged here as we do at home, but there are more different kinds of goods in one shop; and if mamma wishes to buy me a dress, she does n't find a place where they sell nothing but dresses, as in Boston, but where there are many different kinds of other things.

When we get to Princes Street it is the best; on one side the sidewalk is full of people, and beautiful things for them to look at are in all the shops; and on this side, too, are very handsome houses and hotels, which reach all the way from Calton Hill, (oh, Susie, I must n't forget to tell you about this Calton Hill,) to the Castle, though the Castle is not on this street, but on a great hill just above.

One day I went with Jessie's mamma and my mamma, from Princes Street across the beautiful gardens which lie opposite the fine houses, and then they said we were in the Old Town. And it looked old enough! I looked up to the high houses which were before us, and I was almost frightened, they looked so old and high; and after we went up long flights of stone steps we came to a long street which had a great many old houses on it, and churches, too. Mamma said it was a very celebrated street, called the High street, and when I was old enough to read history, I should feel a great deal of interest in it. Only think, these old houses used to belong to very rich people and had beautiful carving and furniture in them, but now the very poorest people crowd into them. It seemed to me, though, as if everybody lived in the street, for it was full. Women were bareheaded and barefooted, and had things to sell, and men were driving teams or drawing little carts, and the poor little children were playing in the dirt. Between some of these high houses are little alleys where the people go into their rooms; but they looked so deep and black I was afraid of them, and I was glad enough when mamma said we would get away from the crowds and go up to the Castle. So we kept on this same street, going up, up, all the time, and it seemed pretty long; but we rested a minute to see all the children go past from the Ragged School. The little girls looked so funny, all dressed alike, with blue dresses and great straw bonnets.

I had a real fright, Susie, when we went into the great Parade before the Castle, for every day, exactly at one o'clock, a cannon is fired, so that everybody can know just what time it is; and then all the gentlemen pull out their watches to see if they are right. But it isn't very nice to be so near such a great gun as we were; and then I kept dreading it, for I heard mamma whisper that it was almost one o'clock. Don't you think it always makes a thing worse to dread it so, Susie? I put my hands over my ears, but I couldn't help hearing it; and oh, dear, how I jumped! I saw some of the soldiers laughing at me.

But when we were in the Castle I liked it. We went over a very deep ditch with some water in it, on a draw-bridge, and then up a steep stone walk with high walls on both sides; and there were so many soldiers, too, everywhere; and when we reached a great broad place, there were great guns, and they pointed off toward the sea. We could look down upon the city, and see all the houses and people, and it was very beautiful. Then we went up higher still, and went into a house, and saw some beautiful gold things in a case: a crown, and a sword, and a ring, and some more. These were called the Crown Jewels, and are worth so much that some one sits by them all the time to watch them. Then we went into another door and saw some gloomy looking rooms, where poor Queen Mary was kept prisoner once, though I do n't know much about it, and her portrait hung on the wall. Oh, it was so beautiful! We went into another building and saw great rooms full of guns and pistols and old armor, such as the soldiers used to wear. We saw some more things, for this Castle is very large and strong, and we waited till it was time for Jessie and Maggie to meet us, and then we all walked home together to dinner.

I wish you had been with us, Susie!

Seventh Letter.

EDINBURGH.

Dear Susie:

When we went to Holyrood Palace, we did n't go through the same streets we did when we went to the Castle, but we turned a little out of the way, so that we could have a good run on Calton Hill. There is a great prison and some handsome houses on one side of it, and on the top are a great many monuments. I wondered if some great battle had not been fought, just as there was on that hill near Boston where Bunker Hill monument is; but Jessie said that some of the most distinguished men of the country had been buried on that hill, and those were their monuments. But on one side, away from the city, there were walks laid out in the green grass, and we had the very nicest place to play "catch"; only we had to be careful and not run onto the white clothes which the washerwomen were all the time spreading out. Was n't it a good place to bleach clothes? Margaret took care of us, and she said that the poor women were allowed a certain part of the grass on that side to dry their clothes.

But it rains so much in Scotland, or it does while we are here, that I shouldn't think clothes would dry very soon. Why, every time we go out, Susie, each of us take a little umbrella for fear it may rain!

After we had chased each other down the hill, we went to the Palace, and I was a good deal disappointed, for it looked gloomy, I thought. But it is in such a pretty place, with green fields behind it, and a great high mountain, called Arthur's Seat, off at one side, and on the other side are city houses, and just before it is one end of that old High Street I wrote you about. The Castle is at one end and the Palace at the other.

I was almost afraid to go past the two soldiers who were marching in front of the door, but Maggie laughed at me, so I took one of her hands and one of Jessie's, and we all went in to the great square, which has the Palace all around it. I wished I knew more about Queen Mary, who used to live there; but Jessie promised to lend me a little book about her, and I am going to read it to-day. Ask your mother, Susie, to tell you about her, too.

We saw a great many rooms filled with pictures and very old furniture; and some of the rooms were very small and had little windows; but I didn't like any of them, and Maggie said she shouldn't like to be a queen, if she had to live there. There were a great many people in Queen Mary's rooms, and we saw her bed, and work-box, and the little fire-place where she had a fire, and on one side of the room hung great pieces of her worsted work. Jessie lifted up one corner, and there was a door, which we could not open, and some one told us that there were the stairs where some wicked men came up and murdered one of the gentlemen who were sitting at her tea-table, when she had company. We peeped into the little room where the company had been that night, but it didn't seem as though there was room enough for people to sit around a table. After we had seen all we wanted to, we thought it would be so nice to go from these old cheerless looking rooms to the other part of the Palace, where are some splendid rooms where Queen Victoria lives when she comes to Edinburgh; but the guards wouldn't let us go in. So we all looked into the old stone chapel where Queen Mary used to go very often to hear the priest, for Jessie said she was a Roman Catholic. I hope it didn't look then as it does now, for the windows are all gone, and the stones are all black with the great fire which burned it, and the ivy is growing all around. I picked some, and perhaps I can send you a leaf in this letter.

I don't think you will like this letter much, Susie, for I can't tell about such things very well. I like to write better about our plays. We didn't play much, though, when we went home from the Palace, for we went through the High street, and we had to be careful and not get run over. A great boy almost knocked

Maggie down when she was just going along on the sidewalk. Oh, you never saw such strange things and such odd looking houses as there are on that street. They run long poles out from the upper windows and hang all their clothes on them to dry. Jessie pointed out one very old house, and said a minister used to live there who talked a great deal to Queen Mary about being so wicked as to be a Roman Catholic, and she was afraid of him. She said his name was John Knox.

We are going away from Edinburgh before long, Susie. I am so sorry!

Eighth Letter.

EDINBURGH.

Dear Cousin Susie:

I am not writing this letter in Maggie's house, because papa said we had made such a long visit that we must go away and find some pleasant rooms, and live as people do when they come to Edinburgh and haven't any friends to visit. Papa says it is called taking lodgings, and people in America don't know much about it; but we think it is a very nice way to live, though I am lonely enough without my little friends. So we have some rooms to ourselves, and the lady we live with buys anything we want her to, and cooks anything for us; and we have our meals in our sitting room by ourselves, and it seems almost as though we were at home again. Almost every night at tea I have a little marmalade to eat with my bread. You wouldn't like it at first, Susie, because it is made of bitter oranges; but by and by you would like it as much as I do, I think. We buy it in little white jars, and I'll try and keep an empty one to carry home.

The butter we have is all fresh, for the Scotch people like it the best; and we have such great loaves of bread that anybody in America would wonder what kind of a plate to put them on. And we make our tea as the Scotch ladies do, they make such nice tea, mamma says. The ladies here pour a litle boiling water on to great deal of tea, and then cover the teapot with something thick that looks just like a hood for it, and then when this has stood a few minutes, they pour on some more boiling water, and then it is ready. I saw a lady do so where I was last week. Oh, I almost forgot to tell you where I was last week.

I said good bye to Jessie and Maggie and Jackie, (though I shall see them again before I go to London,) and went with papa and mamma to see a lady who lives in a little village a few miles from Edinburgh. I like a little village, don't you, Susie? such as we have in America. I mean! This one wasn't much like it, for the houses were all of stone, and the long street which runs through it was very narrow, and there was a high stone wall on both sides covered with green moss. Some of the houses looked pretty, though, for the ivy grew all over the front. Just think, Susie, this is the same kind of ivy that grows in little pots in America in the houses; they have some at my grandpa's.

I had a pretty nice time at this lady's, only I had nobody to play with, and only one or two books to read. The furniture in her rooms was very nice, and in the sitting room the chairs were polished so that if anybody touched them it would leave a mark; and the lady asked me to be very careful of my fingers. I kept forgetting, and then she said she could give me none of her nice jelly till she saw I never touched them. I tried hard not to forget, but I did, Susie, and I hardly got a taste of the jelly. I was so sorry, for it troubled mamma very much to have me so thoughtless; and then the jelly looked so very nice. She was a very kind lady, though, and once she sent me in America a beautiful great wax doll, as large as your pretty one.

When we came back to Edinburgh mamma took me one day to see two more little Scotch girls, and I loved them very much. One was Maggie and the other Mary, and we played tea sets together, and their mamma allowed us to have some real things to eat. But at supper time I drank some strong tea; and I staid all night, and Maggie and I could n't get to sleep till after midnight. I do n't believe that tea is very good for little girls.

But Susie, I can't write any more, and to-morrow I must pack all my doll's clothes, for we are going to London, and we are all going to take dinner at the Crescent, where Jessie lives, and then we shall have to say good bye. Should n't you be sorry, Susie, if you were in my place? When I get to London I shall write you some more letters.

Mamma sends you her love, and I send you a kiss.

Ninth Letter.

LONDON.

My dear Cousin:

I do n't know what I shall tell you about first; for there is so much I shall want to say.

We did n't much think, last summer, Susie, when we were playing together at your house, that I should be in London so soon. I do n't like it yet as well as I did Edinburgh. We had such a cold ride when we came to London, for we were in the cars a whole night and some of the day-time, too. And when we stopped in the station, and saw all the guards, and such crowds of people, I thought we should certainly be lost. And when we rode in a carriage to our rooms, we went through so many streets, and turned so many corners, and heard so much noise that mamma and I thought we should n't dare to walk out much this winter.

But it is very quiet and pleasant here in our sitting room, and the bright coal fire makes the place look so cheerful. Did I tell you, Susie, that everybody here has a fire in an open grate, instead of in stoves, as we do? and in Scotland, too.

I have got my story books and my doll's things all unpacked, and put away in a drawer; and I am afraid I can't play with them much, now, for there are so many places for us to go to, and the days are so short, here, that it is dark almost before we have seen anything. And we don't have any sunshine at all, Susie, but there is a great deal of smoke and fog, and the streets and the houses look very gloomy, I think. The first day after we came here papa took me to walk, and if I should tell you what crowds of people I saw, and how many carriages of all kinds, and how many policemen, you would think my eyes couldn't see right. We kept walking on till we came to a great building, the very largest and the most beautiful I ever saw; and it was made of stone of such a pretty color, and had such beautiful statues and ornaments all over it; and at one end was a great tower with a splendid clock in it. Oh, it looked as though it was all gold, Susie! and there was another tower at the other end, and that was different but just as beautiful. Papa said these great buildings were called the Houses of Parliament, and it was the place where the great men of England met to talk about what was best for the people. Because it was Saturday we could go in; so papa found the office where the tickets are given out, and the policemen allowed us to follow the other people up the great stairs. And there, Susie, it was so beautiful! There were great paintings, and statues, and stained glass windows; and we went into the great hall where the Queen's throne was. Should n't you like to see a real throne, Susie? There were three beautiful chairs, all covered with red velvet; the middle one was for the Queen, and one for her husband when he was alive, and one for the Prince of Wales. Papa said this great hall was called the House of Lords, and he would show me another one called the House of Commons.

So we walked on through beautiful rooms, and when we came to the hall we found it was different from the other, and I did n't like it so well; but papa said it was in good taste, and that the carving was very rich. I sat down a minute in one of the nice seats, but papa could n't give me much time to rest. We went out a different way from the one we came in, and saw a very large hall, with nothing in it, and it did n't look pleasant. Papa said that was the old hall, and a great many people had been tried in courts there, and some kings, too. I am going to have Dickens' Child's History of England out of Mudie's library to read, and then I shall know more about what they used to do there.

When we were on the street again, two or three men and boys ran up to us, and said to papa, "Show you the Abbey, sir?" I could n't think what they meant; but papa said to them, "No, I have been there often before." "Where, papa?" I said. "To Westminster Abbey, which you can see just across the street." I saw then a great, dark looking stone building, as large as three or four churches together, I should think; and papa said some day when mamma was with us, we would go in to see it. I have heard about it before, have n't you, Susie?

Tenth Letter.

LONDON.

Dear Cousin Susie:

Do you wake up as early in the morning as you used to? I have to wake up early, for there are so many noises and shouts that I can't sleep. When we were in Edinburgh, the bugle call in the Castle used to be the first thing I heard every morning before it was light; and now it is the cries of all the people who have anything to sell; and it seems to last all day, too, for there is something being called out all the time. Do you remember, Susie, that little blue book that my uncle Will brought me home from London, called "London Cries"? Well, the people here do look and shout just as they do in that book. Men and women bring along oranges, and apples, and images, and old iron, and scouring stone, and glass ware; and Jew men come with a pile of old clothes on their backs, or a lot of old hats piled one above the other on their heads; and little boys and girls come to sing and dance, hoping somebody will give them a penny, and sometimes very old men and women do this also; and organ men come with their organs and monkeys; but almost the only cry I like to hear or care anything about, is my little water-cress girl's. I call her so because she is a poor little girl who comes along every night with fresh flowers and water cresses, and mamma allows me to give her a penny and buy some cresses. She calls out "water cre-e-sees," in such a sad kind of tone, but she always smiles when she gets her penny.

I have been here now so many days that I am a little accustomed to the noise, but when we walk out I don't like to cross the streets, for there are carriages coming both ways all the time, and when we are crossing over there is almost always a little street sweeper clinging to us, and begging for money. Oh, there are a great many beggars here in the streets, Susie! and they come up to me sometimes, the boys and girls with matches to sell, and say: "Only ha' penny a box, miss; please miss, a penny!" or, "Please good miss, please good miss, a little money, please good miss!"

There is such a pretty place not far from where we live, that I wish you could see, Susie! It is called the Arcade, and it seems like a great many stores all put together, there are so many pretty things of all kinds, and the prices are very cheap, *I* think, but mamma says she shall not buy me many playthings here, but wait till we get to Germany, because that is the country for toys.

Where do you think we all went day before yesterday? Guess the Crystal Palace, Susie, because that was the place. I had been very impatient to go there to see a great house all of glass, and it was more beautiful than I thought it would be. We had to ride a little while in the cars to get there, and then we stayed all day. I can't tell you half we saw! for there were stuffed animals, and trees and flowers brought from other countries, and strange-looking houses, such as people used to live in in other countries, and statues, and all kinds of pretty toys and books, and wild animals, too, all alive, and great halls for concerts, and such a great organ, and so many other things, and all in this great glass palace! Just think how light it would be, all made of glass! I told mamma it looked some like the fairy land I had read about in a story book.

We saw one place where Bibles were sold; and papa bought a German Testament for me to read when we get to Germany, and he bought me a beautiful little glass vase; but I have broken it. Isn't it too bad?

We had some nice dinner there, too, and I was real hungry. It was so nice to eat in such a beautiful place. Papa was impatient to get a seat before the great organ, because there was to be a fine concert, and so many people were there; but I cared more to see Tom Thumb and his family than to hear the organ; for they were going to come out on the platform after the music was through. I saw them all in America once when I was with Mary and Annie; and I was glad I did; for in the Crystal Palace, the gentlemen crowded before me so I could hardly see. But they sung and appeared as pretty as they always do, and I like to see them very much, though papa and mamma said it seemed so ridiculous to see sensible people care for such nonsense. But little children can't be very sensible, can they, Susie? at any rate we do like to see little Tom Thumb and his little wife, don't we?

When we went home in the evening I slept all the way.

ELEVENTH LETTER.

LONDON.

Dear Susie:

It snowed almost all day yesterday, and to-day it is raining, so that I can't go out. I have been playing with my doll, and have sewed a little for her, (my kind of sewing, you know,) and now I don't know what to do, unless I write to you.

I was delighted yesterday when I saw the snow, for I thought everything would look as clean and white as it does at home; but just as soon as the pretty flakes touched the ground they melted in the thick black mud, and helped to make the walking worse than it was before. It seems to me that nothing does look clean in London in the winter time; and the smoke and yellow fog really blackens anything white in our rooms. Why, Susie, we have our white muslin curtains changed every fortnight, for they don't keep clean any longer.

Shall I tell you about the Tower, or the Tunnel, or St. Paul's, or the Parks, first, Susie? for I have been to see all these places since I wrote about the Crystal

Palace. I believe I liked the Parks best, so I will tell about the others afterwards. We do n't live far from St. James' Park, and when it is pleasant, that is, when the sun tries to shine, I go out there to play. It is some like Boston Common, though it is n't all covered with grass, but has a great many little gardens of flowers. There are great trees, too, and a beautiful pond in the centre, with a nice little bridge over it. All the walks have seats for anybody who is tired, but I do n't see many children sitting to rest. Oh, I think I never saw so many children as there are here every afternoon! Just as soon as they are out of school they come here to play all kinds of plays, and they can't get into much mischief, for the policemen are always ready to see it. The grass is very green here, though it is winter, and some poor little children with hardly any clothes on, sit and roll for a long time on the cold, wet grass. I should have the croup if I did so. Because I have no little girls to play with me, I like best to feed the pretty swans and ducks in the pond; and so every time I go, I carry bread crumbs for them; and they are so tame they will come up on the shore and eat from my hand. Oh, would n't it be so nice if you were here, Susie!

Sometimes we walk through this park, to Green Park; that is not so pretty, but it is just beside the Queen's Palace, and then we go on to Hyde Park. That is the most beautiful! and splendid carriages are all the time driving through with very rich people in them, and gentlemen and ladies are riding horseback; and instead of a pond in the middle is a winding river, with such a large bridge over it. We were there one afternoon when the sun was really shining; and it seemed like fairy land, for there were so many people and all looked so happy. Little boys were sailing their boats on the water, and little girls like me were driving hoop; and they seemed to enjoy it more really than the princes and princesses did riding in their handsome coaches.

I had such a surprise one day when we were going home, through St. James' Park. We saw a great crowd of men and women around the gates of Buckingham Palace, and the flag was up, too, so it made papa think that the Queen was coming out to ride. I begged him to stay, too, for I wanted so much to see Queen Victoria, she is called such a good queen; and then I thought she would have such a splendid dress, and look like the pictures we see of queens. So we waited and waited, but a great many carriages came before hers, of people who had been to visit her; and her son, the Prince of Wales, rode by us on horseback, and afterwards his wife. I thought she had a beautiful face, and she smiled and bowed to all the people. But at last the policemen pushed us back, and another great gate opened, and an elegant carriage with four horses came out. There were two men for drivers in front, and two men behind, and they were all dressed alike; papa lifted me up, and because everybody pressed forward so, I knew it must be the Queen. But she did n't look like a queen at all, Susie, though papa said she was. She was dressed like any other lady, only in black, because her husband has died; but she had such a kind face, and looked so good, that I began to love her, and I think I like her better because her dress is so plain when she goes out to ride. There was a little girl with her.

Oh dear, Susie, I have written up all my paper, and have so much more to write! Next time I will certainly tell about the Tunnel and the Tower.

TWELFTH LETTER.

LONDON.

Dear Susie:

You remember I told you when we went to the Crystal Palace, we went in the cars; when we went to the Tower, we had a steamboat ride. It was a dark day, just like all the London days; but papa said I should like to see the great river Thames, and all the great ships and little boats on it. I used to call it the river Thams, until I heard papa pronounce it like Tems, and now I remember the right way.

We had such a nice ride! only I was a little afraid that our little steamboat would be run down by some great ship; and the river looked like a great broad street, only made of water, and all the ships and steamboats and little boats like different kinds of carriages; and there were so many,— some going down, some coming up, and some steering across,— that I wondered how our captain could guide us safely. We had a fine view of some of the great houses, and after a while we saw St. Paul's Cathedral. I knew it must be St. Paul's, because the great dome was just like some pictures I had seen. But, Susie, did you ever read "Rollo in London"? If you have you will not care to have me write much about the river itself, nor anything to be seen from it, because that book makes the story of it much more interesting than my letter can.

When we reached London Bridge, (it is n't the only bridge in London, Susie, but, it is a great bridge called London Bridge,) our boat stopped, and papa said we must walk the rest of the way to the Tower, and then we would have a good chance to see that part of the city; but it was n't a very pretty part, and I was glad enough when we reached the great gate of the Tower. We went through it and then into a little room to get our tickets, where we waited till some more people joined us; then a man came dressed in the funniest kind of style, and said he was our guide. We saw some more guides, and they were all alike, just as the prison keepers used to be when a bad king lived, called Henry the Eighth, papa said.

We followed him through a great stone gate, where something that looked like a great saw with heavy iron teeth, hung just over our heads; and we saw great iron doors that they used to shut up inside of the gate. Oh, we saw some dreadful things! The buildings were all black and gloomy looking, made of stone, and with such little windows; and we went up dark, narrow stairs, and looked into little rooms where prisoners used to live. In one room the wall was

HELEN ON HER TRAVELS.   45

covered with their names and what they had written. And we went into one little room without a window in it; and it was made in the wall, with a little door, too, and that was where a great man called Sir Walter Raleigh used to sleep. He had a pleasanter room to write in, but he couldn't go out of it, for he was kept a prisoner.

There was a great block there, and a great blade fastened over it; and it used to be for prisoners to be killed upon. I put my head down on it, and the knife hung right over my throat, just in the way it did over theirs. We saw all kinds of iron things to torture people with, and I had a pair of thumb screws put on my thumbs, but they weren't screwed tight, but it made me afraid only to see them. There were great rooms full of guns and swords and pistols, and some of them were arranged and hung up in the form of flowers; and the guide explained them all to us. When we started to go into one great hall, I ran back, for on both sides were great horses side by side, and men on their backs covered with steel armor, and with swords in their hands; and I could see some little boys, too. Wouldn't you have hung back, Susie, to see all those dreadful men? But they all laughed at me; for after all they were not *real* men, but only imitation men and stuffed horses. We did see something I liked, though! We saw some beautiful crowns and jewels that the kings and queens of England have worn. I should like to try a crown on my head, for it sparkles so prettily with the gold and the bright jewels; but I do n't understand how one can cost so much money. But if I do n't stop writing about the Tower, Susie, I can't tell much about the Tunnel. I wanted to see that so much, because it would be so strange to think I was in a great tunnel under a river.

When we came to it, we had in the first place to go down very long flights of stairs; and then we saw what looked like a very long tube, large enough for people to walk through; but one half did n't seem to be used. In the middle were little booths full of pretty things, which women try to sell to everybody that passes through. It was very bright, because the gas was lighted; but I should n't like to live day after day in a great tube under a river, and have no light but gas light, should you, Susie? Every woman that we passed would call out, "Please buy, please buy." At each end were little tents with some kind of exhibition in them, and I could hear music; but papa said we should only lose our money, for there was nothing worth seeing in them.

What a funny ending for a letter!

Good bye, Susie.

THIRTEENTH LETTER.

LONDON.

DEAR SUSIE:

I knew you would laugh about my last letter, for the last part was n't very interesting, I was so tired before I finished. I almost wish mamma would allow me to wait till I get home, and tell you what I have seen, instead of writing so many letters. She says I should forget a great deal by that time; and I know I should, because every week I forget some little things I want to write about.

Yesterday was Sabbath day, and I went to church in the greatest church I ever saw. Do you remember I told you I had the promise of going to see Westminster Abbey some time? Papa thought we should like to go there to service, and then we could hear the great organ, besides the minister's sermon; but as we could go there in the afternoon, and could n't to the other churches, we waited and went to hear Mr. Spurgeon in the morning. Did n't you ever hear anybody talk about Mr. Spurgeon, Susie? I think somebody told me that the Americans generally go to see him and hear him preach once, because he is so popular. I do n't know exactly what that means; but perhaps it means that everybody seems to crowd into his church. It was very unpleasant yesterday morning, and we had to ride all the way; not because it rained, though, but because London is so large that we have to ride to a great many places.

We thought we were in good season; but when we went in, the church seemed to be full, and still the people kept coming. It was such a great church, and so many people can sit down stairs, and then there are two galleries, one above the other, and they run around the whole church. The place where the minister stands is just as high as the first gallery, and of course all the people can hear him very well. Papa said he had almost the finest voice he ever heard. You would like to hear all the people sing together, Susie; for they sing as though they enjoyed it. I liked it better than I did the music in the Abbey, for at Mr. Spurgeon's church I could sing, too.

I never felt so strangely in any church as I did in Westminster Abbey in the afternoon, I am sure I do n't know why. It seemed very still and solemn; and though the daylight came in through the stained glass windows, there were a great many wax tapers lighted. All around were white monuments and statues, because a great many people have been buried there; and when it became darker, they seemed to grow whiter in the candle light, while all the dark shadows behind them, and in the great arches, looked blacker and blacker. And when the minister had finished preaching, and the choir began to sing the closing anthem, and we could hear the great organ, I put my face down in mamma's book, and did n't look around any more, but listened to the most beautiful music. Though I was only a little girl, Susie, it was so beautiful I would like to have heard it for hours; and if the organ began to play very loud, so that I would tremble, almost at once would come such soft, sweet sounds, that I would love to hear it again. I think if I live to be an old lady I can not forget the music I heard yesterday in Westminster Abbey.

This morning, for a surprise, the sun was shining when I woke up, and mamma said we would go to see Covent Garden Market. Oh, Susie, I do wish you could see all the things they have to sell there! all kinds of vegetables, such piles and piles of them; those are out doors; and in a great glass house are the most beautiful flowers, and such nice fruit and nuts. Oh, it was such a temptation to see all the oranges and grapes and figs arranged on little tables on each side of us, and to find that the prices were so high that my pennies would n't buy much. But it was a pleasure to see such nice things; and there was so much sport to see all the people buying and selling. Once in a while mamma would allow me to take out my little pocket book, which she bought for me in Edinburgh, and buy something for a penny or two;

and the great market women looked as pleased to get my penny as I did to get their fruit. Papa says that oranges will be coming in more and more every week, and pretty soon there will be boys and girls in every street selling great ripe oranges. I wish I could send you one in a letter.

What kind of a hat has your dolly, Susie? I have forgotten. I want mine to have one, but mamma says perhaps I had better wait till we are in Germany, because the fashions may be different there.

Now I am going to sew; not my way, but mamma's way; and that is so hard.

FOURTEENTH LETTER.

LONDON:

DEAR COUSIN SUSIE:

Papa and mamma have gone out to ride; and because I am so tired I am to stay at home to rest and to write to you. You will wonder why I am tired; but the reason is, I took such a long walk this morning, and went to the top of St. Paul's, besides. I had been into that great church before, but had never climbed to the top. It was rather hard work. Papa said it was ten years since he had done so, and I am sure I should wish to wait ten years before I should do it again.

We spent some time in wandering around, looking at the statues and monuments, and at the great organ and the beautiful carving, and then we went to some stairs in the side of the church, which seemed to be made in the wall. Papa paid some money to the man who staid there; and then we went up, up, till we came to the Whispering Gallery. This is a narrow gallery which runs around the inside of the dome, and seems a very great way up from the floor of the church.

It almost made me dizzy to look down. This is called the Whispering Gallery, because anybody can hear the slightest whisper, or the ticking of a watch, across it. The gentleman who took our tickets sent us to the side of the gallery opposite to him, and told us to put our heads against the wall, and he would put his mouth to the wall where he was, and speak to us. We could understand all he said, and then papa and I tried it, and we carried on a nice little conversation together, though we were so far apart.

Then we began to go up more stairs, again; and we kept on and on, till we lost all light from the little windows, and it was so dark we could not in some places see the stairs; and they were so narrow, too, that if we met people coming down we could hardly turn out for them. But you know my papa is a funny man, and he kept us laughing all the way; and he would tell us what a fine prospect we should have of London, when we were really at the top. So we kept stumbling up; but when we reached the top, and stepped out on the outside platform, we could see hardly anything but a great sea of fog. When we started from home the sun was shining; but by the time we were at the top, the whole air was full of fog, and the sun looked like a little dull red ball. I was disappointed enough, and didn't enjoy the going down as well as the going up. Before we went down, though, we went through a little door at one side of the stairs, and found we were at the very top of the dome in the inside. Oh, it was so high up! The people at the bottom where we had been, walking about, looked like the little Lilliputians I read about once. You know the story, don't you, Susie?

I liked my visit to St. Paul's very well, and I should like to go there on Sunday, and hear that great organ. But I had a better time yesterday afternoon. Oh, it was such a beautiful place we went to! and such beautiful things we saw!

Did you ever hear of a place in London called Madame Tussaud's, Susie? I never did till I came here; but papa says it is one of "the sights" which everybody goes to see; and if people like it as much as I do, I don't wonder! There are a number of splendid halls full of wax people. Mamma called them wax figures; but they looked just as if they were living people. They are made to resemble distinguished people who have lived, and who are living now; and of course they are all very different, because each figure is made to look exactly like some person; and the hair and the eyes and the whole face just as much like life as can be. And then all the people are dressed in the same kind of clothes they used to wear.

We saw all the kings and queens of England, and all the present Royal Family, and all the kings and queens of Europe, too; and all the distinguished men and women of all countries; and some of them had their little children beside them, and there were two or three dear little babies. Some of the gentlemen were dressed like officers, and the kings had splendid robes, and the ladies' dresses were so rich! The people did n't stand up like statues, but were arranged in little groups and companies,— some sitting and some standing,— so that they all seemed to be alive and talking together. Two or three times I was sure they were living men and women. There was a wax figure of President Lincoln there; but it did n't look as good as some others. I wish I could tell you more about it all, for I staid some hours, and then I did n't want to come away. It is called Madame Tussaud's, because she was a French lady, and was the beginner of the collection a good many years ago.

Mamma will come pretty soon, and I want to read a little before she comes.

FIFTEENTH LETTER.

LONDON.

DEAR SUSIE:

I wish I could go to all the nice places that papa and mamma do, and then I should have more to write to you about than I do now; but they often leave me at home in the daytime when they go to visit picture galleries and such places; and in the evenings when they go to concerts and oratorios and lectures, I am in bed, and dreaming about you, sometimes.

Do you remember I told you, that distinguished people were buried in Westminster Abbey? A duke is going to be buried there this week, and there will be a great funeral and a great procession of carriages from his palace to the Abbey. Papa says he was a very rich man, and a very good man, too; and after he died his body was brought from his castle in the country to the palace here, and will lie in state for a few days. I did n't know exactly what that meant, but by special permission we were allowed to go into the palace to see the "Lying in State of the Duke of Northumberland," as it said on our card. The policemen stood at the great iron gate of the palace, but as we had permission they allowed us to go through; and after we had crossed a square, (which has the palace built around it,) we entered a great hall, and a row of servants dressed in black, with wands trimmed with crape in their hands, pointed the way to the room where the coffin was. It was a large room, and it looked very gloomy; for the top and bottom and all the sides were covered with black cloth, and it was only lighted by wax tapers. The coffin was in the centre, and upon it rested the Duke's badges, and his sword and his coronet. At the head of the coffin, hung against the wall in a frame many badges and marks of honor he had received.

The room was so still and black and solemn! It all seemed very different from anything I had ever seen before. When we came out we passed through handsome rooms, and saw statues and beautiful marble stairs; and anybody would have known that some very rich person had lived there. I could hardly believe that the great man who had owned all these nice things was lying shut up in that coffin. It has made me feel very sober, since I came home, and I don't feel much like telling you about the other places I have seen this week.

I have had some very nice times with some little American children who live here in London. Mary, Freddy, and Howard their names are. Howard is just the size of my little friend Walter, at home, and just about as roguish. They don't live very near us, and once I staid all night with them, and the next forenoon I went to their Kindergarten with them. You won't know what that means, perhaps, but it is the name of their school. It is a kind of play school, such as they have in Germany, and I like it very much. Very little children can go, and they learn to make pretty things, and sing nice songs, and the little girls sew. I wish I could go to one in America; but perhaps when we are in Germany I can. Papa says there are a very few now in America, and bye and bye there will be more.

Won't it be nice when I go to Germany, Susie? There will be so many new things to see!

Papa goes every morning to the new reading room in the British Museum to study, and I have been there once to see it. It is the very nicest place for gentlemen to study I ever saw. The desks are so convenient, and it is very light, because all overhead is a dome of glass. Besides this reading room and some great libraries, there is almost everything else in the British Museum; and sometimes mamma and I have spent almost a whole day, wandering around, looking at the curiosities, and the statues, and the stuffed animals and birds, and the precious stones, and the mummies, and so many more things I can not tell them nearly all. Perhaps I can tell more about it next time if I don't forget it.

I can't write many more letters from London, because winter is most gone; and when it is spring we shall go to Germany.

Sixteenth Letter.

LONDON.

Dear Susie:

Papa has just brought me some American apples; they are better than any apples that grow here, and the English people know that, too. Did n't we have nice times eating apples and nuts when I was at your house? Last night for tea we had some American peaches, too; mamma bought them all preserved in a great glass jar, and we enjoyed them very much. There are all kinds of nice things to eat, here, such nice jellies and preserves, and such pretty little china boxes of preserved meats. I like to go into a bake shop, for there are so many kinds of buns and tarts. All the shops here in London are very beautiful; I mean I see more pretty things than I did in Edinburgh, and every time we go out to walk, I want to buy a great many things. Almost all the things in the shop windows have the prices marked upon them, and sometimes things are very cheap, mamma says. I always forget about the money, and think one penny is just one of our cents, but instead of that it is two cents.

If you ever come to London, Susie, and you want to see the prettiest things in the shops, ask your papa to take you to Regent street, and you will like it as well as I do, I think. I can't tell you what nice things there are there, for there are so many; but you must be careful, if you try to cross the street, or you will be run over, there are so many carriages.

Mamma and I were walking along Regent street the other day, because I was going to a German fair, to see children's playthings; and Mary and Freddy told me I could buy ever so many things at a penny apiece. While we were going on, we saw a poor little boy crying so hard; and he looked so cold I did n't wonder he cried. He had n't any hat on, nor any shoes and stockings; and his clothes were full of holes. He did n't beg, but he looked up to mamma as though he wanted something; and she asked me if I would like to give him a penny. It was pretty hard to do it; but he looked so thankful when mamma told him to buy himself some bread, that I was almost sorry I had not given him some more. But there are so many beggars, Susie, that I should not keep one penny if I gave one to all I see; and papa says some of them tell wrong stories in order to get money. I never knew before that there were so many very rich looking people and so many very poor looking people in the world, as we see in London every time we go out to walk.

One day, not long ago, it was so warm and pleasant that papa said he would not go to the British Museum, but would take us to see all the wild animals. That was one of the places I had wanted the most to see, for I had read about the Zoological Gardens in our Guide to London, (that is what the place is called, Susie.) We rode so long before we got there, that I thought we must be in some other city; but papa said it was London all the way.

We staid there almost all day, and I saw all the animals I ever heard of. Some of them, like the birds and the antelopes, were very pretty and gentle, and some like the lions and bears and tigers looked so fierce, I was afraid of them. There was a great house made of glass for the monkeys, and I watched them play together for a long time, and they seemed to know so much that grown up people could'nt help laughing at them. Then there was another house full of parrots. Oh, such a noise as they made, all talking at once! The great bears were out doors in great pens, but they did'nt seem to be cold. I saw a great white bear climb a pole, and papa wondered if he could climb the North pole so well, before he was brought to London. But papa looked so roguish I do n't think he was in earnest. I did 'nt like the alligators nor the great rhinoceros, and I was very much afraid of the large black animal which lives sometimes in the water. Papa called it a hippopotamus. (Have I spelt it right; such a long word?) I saw some animals that I should like for my pets, they were so pretty. I hope you can go there sometime, Susie! What long letters I do write! dont I?

SEVENTEENTH LETTER.

LONDON.

DEAR COUSIN SUSIE:

I didn't write you any letter last week because I had so much else to do. I went shopping with mamma; and I made my doll some new clothes, and I went to visit some Americans who were friends of mamma's, and had some little children to play with; and then all the rest of the time I was trying to finish one of my books from Mudie's Library.

When we are in Germany I am afraid I can't have many English books to read, and so papa gets all he can for me now. Mudie's Library is very large, and has all the new books that are good, papa says, but there are not many for children. I had one book from there that was so nice! It was "Cushions and Corners;" and I wish it was mine to keep.

We are going away from London next week, if the weather is pleasant, and there are some more things for me to see yet. We have been here so long that I am almost sorry to go to Germany, for this seems now like a kind of home, and I like to see so many new things;

and when Sunday comes I like very much to go to the churches here. Oh, Susie, I have seen so many different churches, and seen so many ministers that papa says are very distinguished in America.

The little children here sit very still in church, as still as you used to.

Mamma just peeped over my shoulder and said I must tell you about my going to Greenwich to see all the sailors there. I wish mamma would write about it, but she says these are my letters, and I must tell my stories alone. When we started to go to Greenwich the weather was very pleasant, and I begged papa to go there in a steamboat, so that I could see the river Thames again, and all the fine bridges on it. So we went down in the boat, and came back in the cars; it was so cold that we didn't enjoy it much, and I had to keep my face in mamma's muff, instead of looking at the fine bridges and houses.

But we had a nice time when we were there. There are two great stone buildings, large enough to be palaces, and they looked like them; and sailors who are very old men, who have been on the seas and become infirm, live in them. Some of these old men have been in battles and have lost an arm or a leg. They are all dressed alike; and those we saw looked happy, and seemed to be glad they had such a good home. We went through a great hall, and on both sides of it were little rooms fitted up for the sailors. Each man had a room for himself, and besides the bed and table and chair which were given to him, he was allowed to put any little things he pleased into his cabin. They all call their little rooms cabins; is n't it funny? One old man with only one arm, led me into his cabin and showed me a little ship he had made, and told me stories about the battles he had been in.

We went into great halls and saw things that had been kept which had belonged to great commanders; and we saw a great number of pictures and portraits. What we all liked to see, was some things which men had found which used to belong to Sir John Franklin and his men. Did you ever hear how they were lost? We saw his watch, and spoons and knives that the men had used.

After we had seen all these things, it was time to go to the dining hall, and see the tables spread for the dinner. All the plates were made of tin, and the seats were wooden benches, but everything looked clean. I thought I should n't like their dinner very well; but papa said if I had been a sailor a good many years, I should like plain, wholesome food better than anything else.

This makes me think, Susie, of what a gentleman sent me yesterday: a plate full of raspberry tarts! I can play tea-sets with them, and have enough for tea besides.

This afternoon we are going to some beautiful gardens and to South Kensington Museum, and to-morrow somewhere else; but I don't believe I can write to you about them, I shall be so busy. Won't it seem strange if my next letter is from Germany? We are going to Rotterdam, too.

Eighteenth Letter.

BONN, ON THE RHINE.

Dear Cousin Susie:

We did leave London the week after I wrote my last letter, just as I thought we should, and we have been in Germany three or four days already; but there has been so much for me to see, that I have n't felt like writing any letters. I have been very tired, too, for it was a very long journey from London, I thought; though mamma says a little girl who has crossed the great Atlantic ocean should n't complain of such a short steamboat ride. It was n't the time on the steamboat, that I did n't like; but we had so many changes, and altogether it was n't so nice as I thought it was going to be. What is the reason that very often we do n't have such a pleasant time as we thought we should?

But I'll tell you all about it, and then perhaps you will think it was beautiful, and that you would have enjoyed it very much.

Papa thought he would not go all the way from London to Rotterdam in the steamboat, but would try the new route, as he called it. So about eight o'clock one evening, (that is just my bed-time, you know,) we started in a carriage to ride to the station. The streets in London looked so bright and so pretty, lighted up with gas, that I did feel really sorry to go away. I hope we shall go there again before we go home to America.

There was a great deal of confusion in the depot, because so many people were going in the night train, just as we were; but after a time papa said our baggage was taken care of, and we seated ourselves in the cars, to ride till twelve o'clock. I was wrapped up in a large shawl, and felt pretty comfortable all the time, though I do n't think I was asleep. Mamma laughed about that, and said that little folks do n't always know when they are asleep.

Just about midnight the cars stopped, and we walked a little way to a large steamboat; and there we had a funny time! We could n't have a state-room together, as we always had before, but papa was sent to the gentlemen's cabin to sleep, and mamma and I were told to follow the other ladies to the ladies' cabin. When we found it, everything was very nice and pretty, but I was too tired to look at anything. All the ladies were hurrying to find state-rooms, but the trouble was, there were hardly any ready. There was a new stewardess, and she had n't made all the rooms ready, and so we had to wait and wait a long time. Some of the ladies scolded her; but it did no good. Bye and bye our little room was ready, and it was very nice and cosy, but we found the clean sheet and blankets were very damp; and mamma said I should certainly have the rheumatism if I was undressed. Did you ever hear of little girls having the rheumatism, Susie? But I was glad to go to sleep in any way, so we looked around for our shawls to cover ourselves with, but—now comes the worst of it—papa had forgotten, and kept them and our travelling bag with him, and we did n't know at all where he was. We had a good laugh about it, and then mamma covered me with a great square pillow, and I think I went to sleep.

Papa thought we would want to sleep, so he did n't disturb us; but the stewardess woke us up some time in the forenoon, and said we ought to go up on deck and see the country and the river before we reached Rotterdam.

And oh, it was the strangest looking country when we did see it! We were not on the sea any more, but sailing up a river; and on both sides the shore was near enough for us to see the little houses, and the funny looking people. And all the land was as flat as a floor, almost; there was n't even a little hill; and there were so many great wind-mills. In every direction we would look, were four or five great wheels up in the air, turning slowly with the wind.

I liked to watch the people beside us, as much as I did these other things; for some of them were Dutch people, and some Germans, and they were dressed so oddly, and talked very strangely. Some of them were going to their homes, but they had been long enough in England to learn a little English. They said England was a nice country, but Germany was better still. I wonder if I shall think so!

I think I'll stop now, and perhaps to-morrow write you another letter, before I forget what I want to tell about Rotterdam and Cologne.

Nineteenth Letter.

BONN.

Dear Susie:

Mamma says I can send two letters by one mail this time, so I will commence just where I left off yesterday.

Our steamboat kept going slower and slower, till we stopped; and because the prettiest part of Rotterdam lies along by the side of the river, we had a good chance to see it. And the houses were so neat and white, and the sun was shining so brightly, and the sides of the river looked so cheerful with all the ships, that I thought it was much prettier than London. When we almost touched the wharf, a great many men and boys crowded up to the edge to see us; and you would have laughed to have seen them, though they did n't seem to think at all that there was anything funny about them. They almost all wore wooden shoes, and they were so thick and so large that papa called them boats; and they were really little boats, for they were turned up at the toes like the canoes the Indians make. The boys did n't wear any hats on their heads, and they were dressed like men.

Our baggage wasn't opened here to be searched, but we were allowed to go at once to the depot. It was a low, brown building near by, and didn't look much like our depots at home. And the inside was just as different. There was a first-class room, but nobody went in there; papa says very few people ride first-class in this country, because the second-class cars are just as good as the English first-class. We looked into the third-class room, and that was full of men and women drinking beer and smoking; then we went into the second-class room, and we found some nice people who had come from London the same way we had. There was a little English boy, too, and we had a nice time together, walking about the great room, and looking at the funny things. There were a number of pictures hanging on the walls, and in different parts of the room were glass cases or closets, full of odd-looking china dishes, all kinds of cups and saucers, and pitchers, and some painted china that I can't guess what it could be used for.

After we had something to eat, (I have forgotten what it was,) we all went out to walk a little. Some of the houses were very pretty, and all were just as clean and neat as they could be. I should think the women would have to be cleaning all the time, to make everything look so nice.

Every nice house had a little looking-glass put out from some window in a little round frame, so that the people in the rooms could see who was coming down the street. Wasn't that a nice way, Susie? Some of the shops had pretty things, and we saw very nice pictures; but if we stood long looking at anything, the people would gaze at us, for they knew we were strangers. The people in the streets, even the servant girls, looked as neat as the houses;—but I must stop telling you about Rotterdam, or I can't have room for anything else. Only just about the canals! Instead of streets they have canals of water, and have boats instead of carriages! No, not all, of course, but we saw some streets and as many canals.

We rode in the cars till we came to Emerich, a place just on the border of Prussia, papa said, and then all the passengers had to get out, and go into a room where our baggage had been carried, to see it examined. Every person had to unlock his trunks, and the guards pulled up the things, to see what was in them. Ours were the last ones looked at, and perhaps that was the reason that our things were not disturbed much. We were glad to get our comfortable seats again, and we had some nice companions all the way till we stopped again. Little Frank, the English boy, was in our coupé. We had to stop once in the evening to change cars, and then we got some supper. I had a German pfankuchen, and it tasted some like Aunt Susan's doughnuts, though not so good. Then we rode till we came to Cologne, and the cars didn't go any farther; it was ten o'clock, too, and we were all sleepy enough.

Frank's mother was going to stop at the Victoria Hotel, and we went there, too, because papa didn't know about Cologne very well. We all rode in the omnibus that belongs to the hotel, and it seemed as though we should be turned over, we rode so fast. It was a splendid hotel, Susie, and I had a little bed with beautiful damask curtains all around it, and a little bed of real down to put over me, instead of a quilt.

Oh, dear! I wish I knew how to write letters, and get in all I want to. I shall have to finish this another time.

TWENTIETH LETTER.

BONN.

DEAR SUSIE:

I wish I could commence this letter by telling you what I have been doing to-day, instead of going back a week, to finish the story about Cologne, and our coming to Bonn. I call it a story, because these letters of mine seem some like a long story, when they are put together, do n't you think so?

I believe I had just told you about my nice bed in the Victoria Hotel, when I had to stop writing. It was pretty hard to leave it the next morning, I was so sleepy; but papa had ordered our breakfast early, so that we would have time to walk some before the cars started. We did n't go into a dining room to eat breakfast, but a servant brought some coffee and rolls to our room. In Germany the people do n't eat butter in the morning, but we asked for some.

I could see in the morning what a beautiful room we had slept in, but it was very different from an American room. The stove was as pretty as a handsome piece of furniture, for it was made of beautifully carved iron, and bronzed over, and it did n't look like a stove at all. There were two tall, large wax tapers on the table, in silver candlesticks; and although we had only lighted one, and burned it a very short time, papa had to pay for both of them, and much more than they could cost, too. He says that is the custom everywhere in the German hotels, to make people pay a great deal for the lights, even if they are not used; and that sometimes travellers are so vexed about it that they carry away the wax candles, after they have paid for them.

We have been to see the Dome, or the great Cathedral; and I can not possibly tell you how large it is, nor how grand it looked. It was commenced hundreds of years ago, and is n't nearly finished yet. There are to be two immense towers when it is done, and men are at work upon it all the time; but it seems as though they could never finish. On the top of one of the half-made towers are real trees growing, and there is a kind of machine up there, too, left a long time ago by the workmen, called a crane. Papa played a nice joke upon me. You know there is a great bird called a crane, too; and when he said a crane had been feeding there for years, I looked a long time to see a real live bird, but I did n't see it, of course; though a great many dear little birds have built their nests in the old walls and towers, and keep flying around.

As we walked towards the Dome to go in, a great

many men and boys crowded around us, to show the way, and they clung to us just like burrs; but we found the way ourselves. When we went in, a man came up to us with a plate, for papa to put money in, and then told us where we could walk; because people were there for service, and we must n't go in the middle aisles. All over the church men and women were kneeling and crossing themselves, and the priests were praying, and somebody was playing the great organ; but the inside of the church was so grand and beautiful, I could look at nothing else. There were some strangers there besides us, and the priests watched all of us; and when papa and mamma walked arm-in-arm, one of the priests said that was n't allowed there. Was n't it strange?

After we came out, we had time to walk around the narrow streets, and see the tall, odd-looking houses, and the strange-looking, talking people. There were some beautiful things in the shop windows, and we bought some little pictures, and something else that I liked better: that was, real cologne, Susie. You know we have nice cologne water made in America,— I had a little bottle once,— but this would seem to be much nicer made in Cologne itself, and in the very place where it was first made. Mamma gave me a bottle in a nice case, so it could n't break, and I have n't opened it yet; perhaps I shall not until we go home. I know it is nice, because the lady where we bought our bottles gave me some on my handkerchief.

I should n't like at all to live in Cologne; the streets are very narrow and very dirty. Our guide book says it has the reputation of being almost the dirtiest German city. There are no sidewalks, and everybody walks in the middle of the street, on little paving stones, too, which hurt anybody's feet very much.

The depôt was a splendid great building, and I saw the Queen of Prussia there; she was taking a journey, and had a handsome car to ride in. Mamma and I clung close to papa, for we could n't speak German, and if any one spoke to us, all we could say was, "I do n't understand."

We had a nice ride to Bonn, and then I had to bid good bye to Frank, because he was going with his mother to Frankfort.

TWENTY-FIRST LETTER.

BONN.

Dear Cousin Susie:

It was only yesterday that I wrote a letter to you, but I have no one to play with me now, and I am so lonely that I shall perhaps enjoy writing again.

You would n't think I could be very lonely, if you could be here in the room with me, and look out of the window; for all the street and the square opposite are full of children playing, and they seem so happy, and have so many nice games, that you would like to watch them, I know. But though they make noise enough, and talk very loud, I cannot understand one word they say, for they are Germans. The little girls are dressed very differently from the way we are dressed. The very little ones have their hair long and put up in nets, and they wear long dresses, made in the funniest way, too; and a good many of them stop playing sometimes, and begin to knit. The smallest ones have some knitting work with them, and they do n't seem to drop the stitches, as I do.

All day long I have had enough to see from the

windows; on the other side of the square which I mentioned, is a great Catholic church, (papa says almost all the people here are Catholics,) and men and women have been going in and coming out, all the time since five o'clock this morning. Some of the ladies look like rich ladies, and wear beautiful clothes, and carry little books bound in gold; but most of the people seem to be poor, and a great many of the women seem to be servant girls. They wear nothing on their heads generally, though sometimes a clean white handkerchief is pinned over. All the people look clean, even the little children.

The weather is so warm and beautiful that it seems like summer; and just think, when we left London two weeks ago, it was dark and cold; but the sun shines here all the time. We haven't even had any fire to-day in our funny-looking stove, but have the windows open all day. The windows are not like any I ever saw; they are not opened by sliding them up or down, like ones at home, but open in the middle, and swing into the room like two glass doors; and they are so long they come almost to the floor, so I can step out and lean against the iron railing which is before them. Such pretty white muslin curtains we have, too; and I see them in all the houses; they make the houses look light and cheerful.

I don't know whether you would like this sitting room of ours, or not, Susie; we have no carpet on the floor, (people don't in Germany,) only a little piece under the table; the table is moved up in front of the sofa, so that when we sit at the table to eat, one or two of us can sit on the sofa. We have some very pretty furniture in the room, though it does n't seem very strong; and such a nice writing desk! it is full of little drawers and places for books. I am writing this letter on it now. I miss my little rocking chair the most of everything; and we have hardly seen any kind of a rocking chair since we left America.

We do n't like this street very well; it is very narrow and noisy. It is one of the streets that lead down to the Rhine, and carriages and teams are passing constantly. On each side of the street is a gutter of dirty water, just as in all the streets in the city; and as there are no sidewalks, every time we go out to walk, we must go in the middle of the street, on the little hard stones.

I was n't with papa and mamma when they engaged these rooms. I was so tired that I staid on the sofa in the depôt, and I had a very pretty room to be in and something good to eat; and the guard man was very kind to me. When he went out he locked the doors, because he did n't allow people to go into the first-class room without him. I did n't like to be locked in very well, but the doors were made of glass, so that I could see out; and when the trains came past, I liked to watch them. The engines are very different from the American ones; the engineer and fireman have no little house to stay in, and the trains have many more cars than ours. So many people are travelling up the Rhine, and very few come from Cologne to Bonn in the steamboat, because the scenery is not pleasant on that part of the Rhine, papa says.

I had to stay a long time alone; but when papa came for me, he told how many rooms he had looked at first. It is hard now to get rooms here, because the students are just coming back to the University to study.

I had a nice ride in a German carriage to this street, and I have had a nice time ever since.

Twenty-Second Letter.

BONN.

Dear Cousin Susie:

I don't have at all the same kind of places to visit here that I did in London, but I like living here better, and have enough that is new to see. I am trying to learn a little German from papa, and I can say a few easy words now to Marie, our servant girl. She always laughs when I try to say anything, but it is such a good-natured laugh, that I don't mind it. She is so kind that I really love her; and sometimes she takes me to walk, and then she tells her friends I am a little American girl.

Oh, Susie, I was so mortified yesterday! I went out alone to a shop very near here, to buy something for mamma; she told me just what to say, and I kept repeating the funny German words all the way; but when I went into the shop the people couldn't understand me, and I couldn't understand them; so I ran home crying. I know that was silly, but I thought I couldn't help it.

Every morning after breakfast we take a walk, and

now we have seen most of the streets of Bonn. I mean by that, we have seen all the part within the walls. There used to be a great stone wall around the city, but now it is almost all gone; only the great gates still remain. Some of these are very handsome, and some are very high and strange-looking; but beyond these gates the walks are beautiful. There are the finest streets and the most elegant houses, with fine gardens, too, sometimes, and long rows of trees, and sidewalks. I think papa will find us some rooms on one of these streets, and then I shall be very happy.

Bonn seems like a small city, but the houses are packed so closely together, and the people are crowded so closely together in them, that there are a great many living in this little city, papa told me to-day. The streets are narrow, though quite clean; and there are no trees at all, and no sidewalks; or if there are any, they are too narrow for more than one person.

Every time we walk out the people gaze at us, and so do the market women, too, when we ask them any questions. Oh, I must tell you how pretty the market places do look! We go often to see the women, and what they have to sell, when it is early. They sell their things out of doors, and on the great squares, which are surrounded on every side by buildings. The market women are dressed so funny, and all about alike. They wear blue calico dresses made very short, and brown stockings, and very thick, stout shoes. Over their heads they have pinned a large linen cloth, as white as snow; and you can imagine, Susie, what a pretty sight it must be when two or three hundred of them are together, and the sun is shining down upon their white heads. They have all kinds of vegetables and flowers, (of course I mean all those they can get at this time of the year, and it has been so warm that many things are ready for market,) and arrange them in rows in their baskets. Fresh butter and eggs, too, are plenty. At first I used to pity them when I saw them bring their great loads of things to market, for they carry everything in baskets on the top of their heads; and sometimes we have seen women carrying two or three at once, and full, too. This is the way in which they carry everything, I believe, excepting water, for they carry baskets of wood and clothes in the same way; but they look very contented and happy. I wish you could see the washerwomen carry home to ladies their clean clothes. They have a basket full on their backs, and have their shoulders covered with such things as must be starched, skirts and dresses; so they look like poles hung all around with clothes.

When we see all we want to in the morning, papa and mamma go home to study, and I to read and play; though at dinner time we have to go out again to a hotel, because the people in this house do n't cook our dinner for us. I do n't like what we have to eat very well, but papa says this is thorough German; our soups are white and thick, and the meat is cooked in the funniest way, with vegetables, and we do n't see any pies at all, but have some strange kinds of pudding instead. All the German men drink wine or beer instead of water. I tasted some beer the other day, but it was so bitter I could hardly swallow it.

But mamma says I have written long enough, and I may go to walk now. How I wish you could go with me!

TWENTY-THIRD LETTER.

BONN.

DEAR COUSIN SUSIE:

Did n't I write to you, that I hoped papa would find us a pleasanter home on one of those pretty streets outside of the gates? Well, he has done so, and two or three days ago we moved. I called it a real moving, for it is a good deal of trouble to pack all my books and doll's clothes; but then mamma has the hardest part to do, of course.

We have a very pretty place and house to live in now. It is on a street which runs from Bonn towards Coblenz, and there are fine houses on both sides; and we only have to go a very little way before we can see the beautiful river Rhine. Our landlady provides our dinners in our sitting-room; so that we do not have to go out in the middle of the day, and the weather is so very warm,—though it is only Spring,—that no one likes to go out at noon-time. The furniture in our room is very pretty, but it looks as though it would break if we touched it; and we can see that some pieces have been broken off, and then glued on again.

There is a nice little foot-stool here just right for me to play with dolly, but every one of the four legs is fastened on with glue, so I hardly dare to touch it. Papa says it is very generally the case in the towns along the Rhine, that the furniture is so lightly made that it will easily break, and then the lodgers must pay double what it cost.

Mamma and I had a funny time yesterday when we went out shopping. There are beautiful shops here of pictures and carved wood-work, and there is one great shop full of the prettiest porcelain things. I wish we could buy some to carry home, but I suppose they would break. Mamma found she could n't understand well enough to go into the shops where German was spoken, so she inquired where she could find English spoken. There every thing was very pleasant, all but the prices. The shop ladies were very polite, but things cost a great deal. We have heard since that is the way they do every where in Germany, if they see the customers are English or American. Mamma bought me a travelling dress, and she had to pay almost twice as much as it was really worth; and she did n't know the German money very well, and made some strange mistakes.

They have nice places here. I do n't know what they are called in English, but the German people call them conditorein; they are very nice great rooms fitted up with little tables and chairs, and people go in and eat cake and drink a cup of coffee or a glass of wine, and then they are allowed to read the papers. Papa sees the newspapers in one of these, and I went with him once. I don't like the German cakes very well; they only taste good when they are dipped into tea, and this is the only way they are eaten; but we get nice bread, and tender little white rolls, and there are several different kinds of them.

Oh! you would laugh to see the peasant boys and girls carrying home their bread; it isn't white, but black and sour, and is made in long rolls, as long as papa's arm. It is very cheap, and they eat it with cheese and beer. The other day I saw a woman with five or six of these long loaves, and she looked as though she had an armful of wood.

Mamma has bought a little tea machine, so that she can make her own tea. There is a little alcohol lamp which belongs to it; there are a great many pretty bronze and brass and tin machines for making tea. Mamma makes ours, because the German tea is not good; they make it so very weak that even you or I could drink it, and then they put a few drops of rum into every cup.

Mamma has been to several shops to find pure tea, but it all seems to be mixed with herb leaves, which spoil the taste. Papa says if the Germans cannot make good tea, they certainly can good coffee, for he never drank such nice coffee as he finds in Germany. People here don't shut up the tea in tight tin boxes as we do, but do it up in thin papers, or allow it to remain open on plates. It is no wonder it is n't good, is it?

Papa and mamma are talking of sending me to a German school to learn German; it is n't a Kindergarten, but a school where some English scholars go. I shall dread it, for I shall be so lonely; and then I can't have so much time to walk and play.

Last night we had a beautiful walk along the banks of the river Rhine, and saw the steamboats going up and coming down.

Do you like my letters, Susie? Please tell me if you do n't.

Twenty-fourth Letter.

BONN.

Dear Susie:

I almost wish I had a copy of the letters which I write to you, so that I could see what I have written about and what I have not; for as soon as I have sent a letter, I forget what was in it. I wish I could see you when you read my letters. Do you go out on the piazza to sit, and let your dolly hear them? Oh, I think I would almost be willing to go away from Europe, if I could only have one more of those nice walks with you and aunt Susan. I wish everybody was as kind to little children as she is!

I have n't told you anything yet about our Sundays here, have I? You would n't think there was any such day as Sabbath day, if you were here and saw the people walking and riding, and filling the pleasure gardens full, and drinking and smoking there.

The people almost all stop working, only the shop-people generally keep the shops open, and they dress in their best clothes, and try to have a very gay time. Some go away in the cars to some other town to visit their friends, and some hire carriages and take rides, and some have company in their own houses. When we were walking through a beautiful park last Sunday on our way to church, I saw so many little children dressed in white, with wreaths on their heads, that it seemed almost as though I was in America on Fourth of July.

Papa says a great many of them go to church for an hour or two, and then they do not think it at all wrong to do what they please. We go to a Scotch church, and it is almost like a little meeting at home. There is a very nice minister; his name is Dr. Graham, and all the children love him. His house and the church are built together, and so at first papa was puzzled to know where to go; for the building looks some like a church.

But now we go there every Sunday, and there are two or three more Americans besides us, and a number of English and Scotch families. I have seen some dear little children, and I hope I shall become acquainted with them. Papa says there are a great many English families living in Bonn, but most of them go to the English church; we have been there, too. First the Germans who are not Catholics have a service there, and afterwards the English.

Dr. Graham has a great garden behind his house, and has some bee-hives, and a nice swing, too; he asked me to come and swing a little, and perhaps mamma will allow me to go.

It is rather hard for me to write to-day, for I am a little tired. I didn't go to bed very early last night, and I must tell you the reason.

I had almost the best time yesterday that I ever had in my life. Dr. Graham came to see us in the morning and invited us to go with a little party on an excursion. We were to have a steamboat ride and then walk two or three miles to an old ruin, where we would have something to eat, and have time to rest. He said, "be sure and bring your little daughter, and if she is not old enough to walk so far, she can ride on a donkey's back." I was so delighted, and mamma said I might go. She put on me my Scotch winsey dress, and we all carried thick shawls, because we were coming home by moonlight, and it would be cold on the river.

All the party were at the boat in season, and there were two boys and two little girls to be with me. Oh, we had such a beautiful steamboat ride! We sat on deck, and could see the beautiful houses and places on the banks of the river, and some old ruins of castles farther away. The people on the boat were all Germans but our party. We stopped at a little village very near the great ruin called the Drachenfels, and left the boat. Then we had such a merry time. We all walked a little way, and then Dr. Graham put us children on donkeys. I had a nice seat, something like a little chair, to sit in on my donkey's back, and it was covered with red flannel. He was a real naughty donkey: he would go just as he wished to, and sometimes he would turn around so suddenly as almost to throw me off. But then his master would whip him. It was such a nice ride. We climbed up steep paths and through vineyards, and little peasant children would follow us, and offer us flowers for a groschen, that is their money, about as large as an American cent.

The gentlemen and ladies walked, but we all got to the old ruin about the same time. Then we played in the green grass and picked wild flowers, and had some tables spread under the trees, and had some coffee to drink and bread and butter to eat. There was a little house there where people lived who made our coffee and sold us the bread. We played around the old ruin, called the Heisterbach, and then went back. My donkey ran all the way down the hills.

Now you see why I went to bed late!

TWENTY-FIFTH LETTER.

BONN.

DEAR SUSIE:

I shall have to write all my letters now in the afternoons, because I have commenced going to school in the forenoons. I do n't have very far to walk, but I go down this street past the beautiful park and the great hotel to the Coblenz gate, (this is the prettiest gate in Bonn, I think,) and then keep straight on through one of the narrow streets to my school.

It is n't a great school-house where I go, but it is a lady's home, and she has one room for a school-room. She is a very pleasant teacher, but she can't speak any English; all she can say in English is to count one, two, three, four, and so on. She calls me Helene, and tries to make me like the school, but she tells all the children, even the English ones, to talk with me in German, and so, because I can't understand German, I do n't talk with anybody, and I feel very lonely. I suppose she does this because she knows papa wishes me to learn the language.

We have rather a pretty school-room, but we have

uncomfortable wooden seats, and they are not painted. Our teacher teaches the children to read and count and sing and such things, and tells stories in German, and then she gives us a long recess, and we play in her garden.

I do n't play much, though, for the boys and girls play so many games I do n't know, and so I sit alone and look on. There is one dear little boy there I begin to love; I wish he was my little brother. He has long curls and his name is Victor. We do n't talk together, but we smile to each other. I told papa about him and his name, and he says he is the son of a distinguished German poet who died two or three years ago.

I can hear some funny noises in our street, so I will stop writing a little while and look out of the window.

Well, Susie, I have been looking into the street for half an hour, I think, and there is something nice to see all the time. Students go by with funny colored little caps on their heads; and peasant women, with great baskets full of things; and companies of soldiers; and carts with women or dogs harnessed into them; and splendid carriages with rich people; and donkeys with peasant boys driving them; (you would laugh to see these boys take out their colored pocket handkerchiefs, and dust their boots before they go into the city;) and a great many people walking. Oh, I can't tell you nearly all there is to be seen! On the other side of the street, just opposite to our house, is a large garden, filled with old trees; and in the middle of it is a walk which leads to an old house. There is an old lady who comes out of the house every day, and walks up and down this walk; she dresses very oddly, and does n't look as though she cared as much for the fashions as some ladies do; but all the nice-looking people who come past bow very politely to her, and show her great respect. Mamma and I have liked to watch her; and yesterday we heard that a great German poet (not Victor's papa, though,) used to live in that house, and that this old lady was his wife. The Germans were very proud of him, and now they love her. Sometimes a fine carriage, which belongs to some rich people here, comes for her to ride.

We went all of us, yesterday, to the cemetery where this great poet was buried. His name was Mr. Arndt. A German cemetery is very pretty. All the grave stones are made in the form of crosses, and have beautiful ivy twining over them. We saw some beautiful statues of marble, and papa said very good men were buried under them; but I do n't remember their names. There are very pretty little words engraved on the crosses over children's graves: they do n't say they have died, but have "fallen asleep," or "gone home;" that is, German words which mean that.

I wanted to tell you about another walk we took to a church which is on the top of a high hill a little way from Bonn. It is called the Kreutzberg; that is, the Cross Mountain. The church is a Roman Catholic one, and we saw some images and pictures and flowers in it. Then we called a monk to show us a flight of marble stairs, in another part of the church. They are called holy stairs, because they are just like some at Rome, which some people believe Jesus Christ came down; and nobody is allowed to go up those we saw, only by creeping up on their knees. Papa had to give the monk some money, and then we walked around to see the beautiful images on the hill, which the people pray to.

But I have n't any more time, now, Susie.

My birth-day comes very soon!

Twenty-Sixth Letter.

BONN.

Dear Cousin Susie:

Sometimes I wish I was a young lady! Don't you wish you were? Papa and mamma went to a party last evening, but I couldn't go. They were invited to a Professor's house, where they had a German supper; and if you had heard mamma tell me what a German supper was, you would have thought just as I did, that it was almost nicer than Thanksgiving dinner. I hardly ever heard of so many kinds of good things, and all to be eaten at one meal!

But I have been very happy twice this week. One time was when I went with a party of people to a pretty place; and the other was on my birth-day. Papa had promised me one treat better than all the rest, and that was, that I might choose some nice place for us to go on that day. So I took our guide book and read about several favorite places near the Rhine, and at last decided to ask papa to go to Rolandseck, because that seemed to be the most beautiful ruin. But I will tell you about that last, after I have told of the party excursion.

One afternoon papa and mamma were going with a large number of English people in the cars to Godesberg. That is the name of an old ruin a few miles from Bonn; and when mamma heard that several children were going, she allowed me to go. There is a beautiful village there, and some of the houses are very fine, and have great gardens around them, much prettier gardens than I ever saw in America. Rich people who live in Bonn and Cologne in the winters, go to this pretty place to stay in the summers; and sick people go there, too, I believe. After we had walked about the streets, and seen the houses, and the beautiful flowers and trees in the gardens, we started to go up to the old ruin. It wasn't a very long walk, so we didn't need any donkeys. I went between two little girls, and we crossed a little bridge over a brook, where some German women were washing clothes. Then it seemed as though we had left all the nice houses and gardens on the other side; for the rest of the way were little cottages, which looked very dirty, and not pretty at all. We kept going up and up a steep hill, and not up a straight road, either; but it wound around the hill, so that we had a nice chance to get views of the little village, and the country, too.

When we reached the top we went through some stone arches; and it seemed as though we were in houses of stone, with the walls partly fallen down. That was once a strong castle, papa told me, and people went there to get protected if their enemies came against them. Some of the broken walls are very thick and high, and have green ivy growing over them, and sometimes trees and rose bushes. In the middle of all is a great stone tower, thirty feet high. There are no windows in it; only once in a while a little hole to let the light through. We went to the very top of it, and then we could see the Rhine, and the mountains, and Bonn, and as far as Cologne. The Cathedral looked like a black cloud low in the sky.

After we went back to the village, we had a supper around a long white table in a garden. We had some bread and butter and coffee, just what all of us children liked. These gardens that I tell you about, all of them, have little white tables and chairs in them, where people sit to drink coffee or beer. I have seen a great many of them since we came to Germany. Did n't we have a nice time?

But this was n't as good as my birth-day excursion. I had some little presents, too. One was a German story book, for I can read a little German now; and I had a wreath of pink flowers for my head. We went, papa and mamma and I, in the steamboat, to the most beautiful place I ever saw. It was to Rolandseck, (I chose the place myself, you know,) where there is a pretty old ruin; and on the other side of the river is another one, called the Drachenfels, (that means in English the Dragon's Rock,) and just in the middle of the river was such a beautiful island, with a large white house at one end of it. Some nuns used to live there. Was n't it a pretty place to live? Papa cut me down a May-pole,— because, you know, my birthday is in May,— and fastened my wreath to it; and then we had such nice plays.

I gathered my lap full of ivy leaves, and some little girls came up to us with bouquets of wild flowers to sell. Oh, I forgot to tell you that the lily of the valley, that pretty little white flower, grows wild here in the woods. I could n't play long with my leaves, without wanting to jump up and look at the beautiful things all around us. I did n't know before that the world was so beautiful! Do n't forget, if you ever come to Europe, to came here if you can; and then you can go to Rolandseck and see the ruins, and the river Rhine, and the pretty island, and all the little villages scattered around. You will find such beautiful arbors; and very often you will see along the roads and paths, wooden images of Jesus on a cross, or sometimes a cross alone. These are where the people kneel and pray, as they are going through the country; because, you remember, I told you they were, Roman Catholics.

I have n't written a very good letter this time. It was all so nice for me to see, but I can't make it seem so pretty to you! I wish you could see some of the girls I know here. Who do you play with, now I am gone?

TWENTY-SEVENTH LETTER.

HEIDELBERG.

Dear Cousin Susie:

You will see that I can not write any more letters from Bonn. When I wrote the last one I thought we should stay there some time longer; but we were there only two weeks. I didn't seem to get any time to write again, for I went to school and to so many other places. But I think Heidelberg is a much prettier place than Bonn was, and I hope I shall have some nice things to tell you about. We came yesterday, and so I can't write much this time, only about our journey.

You have heard, have n't you, how much travellers like to go up the Rhine? I do n't wonder they do, for we had such a beautiful time! We were on a great steamboat, and the weather was so warm that everybody sat on deck, though there were nice cabins down stairs. A great awning of cloth was made over the deck, so that the sun could n't shine upon us. The first afternoon we went as far as Coblenz; and because it was only the first of the evening, we had time to see the great fortress on the other side of the river, and the bridge of boats which crosses the river, before it was my bed-time.

The next morning we had to take our breakfast in a hurry, because we wished to take the morning boat; but our hotel was very near the river. I wanted very much to buy some nice fresh cherries which we had seen the evening before; but the woman who sold them wasn't up so early, perhaps, for we couldn't find her. But I found afterwards that cherries were sold on the steamboat, though papa had to pay a great deal for one saucer full.

It was very cold sailing up the river so early, though it was warm enough before night, and all the people were wrapped up as though it was winter, and I had on my winter cloak, and even then my teeth chattered. But there was too much to be seen for us to mind the cold much. It was so pleasant to watch all the different people as they came on to the boat. There were some French and English people, and a great many Germans; and some of the English people tried to get the best seats. Then the great Fort and Coblenz looked so pretty in the morning sunlight; and when the steamboat began to move, it was nice to hear the captain give his orders, and to see how the bridge of boats opened for us to go through, and to watch the great wheels turn in the water.

And then all the way from Coblenz the things on the shore began to be prettier and prettier. There were great black castles high up on rocks; and beautiful hills with the sides covered with vineyards, where the funny-looking peasant women were at work; and little villages just on the very edge of the river, and nice roads that seemed to run along on the top of stone banks or walls; and then it was so pretty to watch for the new surprises. I mean by this, Susie, that the river Rhine is so winding that a great deal of the time we could n't tell what next we should see, till we would turn a great bend in the river, and then there would be beautiful palaces, or old castles, or something as fine. I should think it must be pleasanter to go *up* the Rhine, than *down*, on a boat; because going up we must sail more slowly, and so have time to see the things better. Every few minutes we met some great steamboat or little boats; and once we saw a great raft, so large that there were even little log houses on it, and a great many people, too, who lived in them; that is, they slept in them and hung their clothes in them. Papa said they were going to take all the timber that the raft was made of, to some great city down the river, and sell it.

Would you believe it, Susie, that when there were so many new and beautiful things to be seen all the time, that some people would n't mind anything about them? A number of people, to be sure, sat reading their guide-books and watching the old castles; but all the French party, and some of the English, seemed to care more about something good to eat than anything else.

When they first came on deck they ordered a simple breakfast; and in the middle of the forenoon they ordered another nicer one; and they sat at their table, eating, and drinking wine, for a long time. They had as many different kinds of food for their breakfast as you or I would ever get at dinner. While they were eating and talking, I remember we passed a strange-looking old castle in the middle of the river, called Bishop Hatto's Tower. Do you remember the story? He was a bad man, and wouldn't feed poor people in a famine, when his own barns were full; and so an army of rats began to eat them, and then came after him. He was so frightened that he fled to this place in the river, but they followed him, and I think ate him up. I have the story at home in a red book.

When we reached Bingen, most of the people left the boat. It looked so pretty there that papa was almost sorry we were not going to stop, too, and go on to Heidelberg in the cars; but our baggage was marked for Mannheim. So we kept on, but there was nothing more pretty to be seen, only a flat country. We had some dinner on the boat, then mamma and I went down to the ladies' cabin and had a nap.

We stopped one night in Mannheim, and came here in the cars yesterday forenoon.

Twenty-Eighth Letter.

HEIDELBERG.

Dear Susie:

We have the prettiest home here that we have had since we left America. The house we live in is a great handsome house, on the street which leads up to the Castle. It looks much nicer than any other house on the street, on the outside; but the inside is prettier still. The halls are large, and as neat as wax, and the rooms are so pleasant. Our rooms are up two flights of stairs, and I wish you could see them. I cannot tell which is my favorite. Our sleeping room is very large, and is carpeted almost all over; and from the windows we look out upon a most beautiful grove, which is on a great hill in front of the house. The trees are so large, and the grass is so green, that I never get tired looking at them. From our sitting room windows (our sitting room is just the other side of the entry,) we can see the little garden back of our house, and the whole city of Heidelberg, and the Neckar river, and the great hills beyond. We can see the sunset, too, and sometimes just a glimpse of the Rhine.

Oh, this is a beautiful house, and the people who live here are so very kind! A German lady owns the house, and her daughter lives with her. She is such a pleasant lady! She has been in England, too, so that she can speak English perfectly. There are a number of strangers in the house besides us, and some Americans are coming next month; and a Scotch family have several rooms on the first story. We have our breakfast and tea in our own room; but we take our dinner in the great dining room, with the others, and we have very nice food. It doesn't seem like any German dinners we have eaten before. If you were only here, we would be so happy together!

Our landlady has a little black dog, and he likes me, so that sometimes when I walk through the city with mamma, he follows us. There is one long street which runs through the city in the same direction that the Neckar does, and there are a great many funny things to be seen on it. At one end of it is the market place, and I like to go there to see the market women sell their things. They don't dress like the market women in Bonn, and they speak a different kind of German, too, so I can hardly understand them. Although it is only June, yet the peasants bring in every day baskets full of cherries and plums and berries. You never saw such great cherries, nor so many different kinds! They are delicious! I wish I could send you some. There are no peaches here, but there is a kind of fruit which looks much like them, and tastes like them, too. These are apricots; but they are not as juicy as peaches. Doesn't your mouth water to read about all these these nice things? I see baskets full of tender green salad every day, and we have it every day for dinner. People don't allow it to grow up and get old, as some people do in America, but they keep it new here, and cut it very often.

I wish you could see the German pumps! I don't know what made me think of them just now, but they are such strange-looking things. They are in every street, because people here do not have water carried into their houses, but the servants have to carry it in pails from the street pumps. They are very tall,— much taller than papa,—and have an iron handle, with a great knob at the end of it, and it swings slowly back and forth, instead of pumping up and down, like our pumps. I tried to pump a little water once, but I couldn't. The handles are very heavy, and the water comes so slowly that anybody must wait a long time to fill a pail. Sometimes servant girls carry tubs of clothes to them to be rinsed, or fish to be washed, or lettuce or vegetables to be prepared for the table. They do have such strange ways of doing things in Germany! I don't believe I ever told you about the cows that I saw in Bonn harnessed or fastened to ploughs. Just think of a cow dragging a plough, and a funny-looking one, too, and a woman managing both of them!

Yesterday we visited the old Castle. We had to

go up this street to get to it, and it is going up hill all the way. On both sides are the oldest looking houses, and the people seem to live in the street. Women were sitting on the steps, and children were playing in the dirt. Sometimes they would come up to us, to offer us flowers, or to beg. Papa says that thousands of people go up and down this street every summer, some on foot, and some in coaches. I should like to ride up in a carriage, but I should n't like to ride down so well, because the way is so steep and so narrow. But the drivers make it safe. They put wooden shoes or drags on the wheels, so that they cannot turn, but drag all the way down. I would rather be on my own feet, would n't you?

I will tell you about the Castle when I write next time.

Twenty-Ninth Letter.

HEIDELBERG.

Dear Susie:

I have had several nice walks lately, and have been to the top of some mountains near here, where we had such fine prospects that we could see for miles. I should like to tell you about one of them; but I promised to tell you about the Castle, did n't I? The old ruins of castles that I saw near Bonn were not much like this one here. This is so large and so beautiful, and it has so many statues and towers, and they look so pretty, with the ivy growing over them. The ivy grows here under our feet, and twines up the trees, and over the old walls. Some parts of the Castle are very old, and the walls are broken and crumbling away; and some parts have been injured by lightning; and there is one tower larger than all, which is broken in the middle, and the top has fallen off. Great trees and bushes are growing now on the top of it; and people can go up there and sit. The newest part of the Castle seems to be built on a precipice, which looks down upon the city; and there is a beautiful stone balcony there, where people walk. The newest parts, some of them, are not spoiled, and the rooms are just as they used to be, and some people live in them now. We went through the inside of all the buildings we could. We saw a chapel, and great halls, and a dungeon, and some old great kitchens; and then we climbed up some long dark stairs in a tower, and went to the very top of it. It was the highest tower of all, and we could see a great distance away. Papa explained to me who the great noble people were who used to live here, and told me how these old rooms I saw, that have no roof to them now, used once to be full of gay ladies and gentlemen. I saw a great oven or an open place at the bottom of a large chimney, where oxen used to be roasted whole. But it is of no use, Susie, to try and describe all I saw. I can't do it! All around the castle are beautiful gardens and woods, and trees have been brought here from all parts of the world.

There are smooth walks in every direction, and pretty white seats for people to rest, and enjoy the views of the city, or the old Castle, through the trees. In one part of the woods, near the Castle, is an open space, and a large square filled with white tables and chairs; and there is a pretty kind of Swiss house, too, where people can go to drink beer or coffee, or order anything to eat. There are concerts here in this place every week, and the people come and listen to the music while they are sipping their coffee. Papa took me with him once, and we had a little table to ourselves. I was hungry, so I had some bread and butter to eat. It was so warm I took off my hat, and so did the ladies, some of them. All the ladies had some nice sewing or some knitting work in their hands, and worked very busily. I thought it was a very pretty sight; and every body looked so happy, and talked so fast, though the moment the band began to play, not a person was allowed to even whisper. One night when I was n't with papa and mamma, they had some trout to eat there. An American gentlemen ordered some and they were brought fresh from the water. I asked papa to get me some, but he said they could only be caught with a *silver* hook, in Heidelberg, and so they were not caught very often.

I am tired telling so much about the Castle; what can I write next? I have become acquainted with William, the little Scotch boy, who lived in the house with us, and we have nice plays together in the garden, and Caro, the dog, plays with us. I hope we shall stay here a long time, and if I was n't an American girl I should like to live here always. But I want to go back to America again, to see you, and grandpa, and Aunt Susan, and my uncles, and my old playthings, too! Did you know I left a little bureau full of books, and toys, and doll's clothes? William has been in Switzerland, and has some very pretty toys. I can hear him calling Caro now; and if mamma is willing I am going to play with him.

Thirtieth Letter.

HEIDELBERG.

My dear Susie:

It is almost too warm to write a letter, or it would be if I were anywhere else in Heidelberg than in our cool sitting room, I think. Our house is on the side of such a high hill, and our rooms are so large, that we seem to have a cool breeze here all the time. But if you could look down upon the city, from the window where I am writing, you would think it looked very hot. The streets are narrow, and have no trees, and the houses have no blinds.

We cannot see many churches, for there are not many in Heidelberg to be seen, and those few don't look much like our churches at home. I went the other day with mamma and Miss Zimmerman, (she is the lady we live with,) and William and his sisters, into the old Roman Catholic Church here, to see some ceremonies. They have them once a year, but I don't know what for. There was a procession of little girls dressed in white, with green wreaths on their heads, and leaves and flowers in their hands; and they walked around the inside of the church, scattering their flowers on the ground. Then a procession of priests and bishops, dressed in the most splendid robes of silk and gold, with something on their heads that looked like crowns, followed them; and over one man, who was dressed the handsomest of all, four boys carried a beautiful silk canopy, and two other boys walked under it, too, each of them carrying a silver dish full of fire, I thought it was, but mamma said it was incense. Little clouds of white smoke kept rising from them all the time. Very often all the procession would stop and repeat prayers, and kneel and make the sign of the cross, and do a great many things that I didn't understand at all. The priests blessed the people, and they seemed to think their priests were as holy and good as they could be. Perhaps the Roman Catholics do this in America, but I never saw them, and so I have told you about it.

Because I have been writing about the churches here, it has made me think what sweet music we heard from the tops of some of the churches yesterday. You will wonder what I mean; but yesterday was Sunday, and it was the anniversary of the Reformation, too. If you don't understand that, ask Aunt Susan to tell you about it and Martin Luther. So the bands of the city went up to the top of the churches, where there is a little kind of gallery made on the outside, and played the sweetest music, some of Luther's music, too. It was just at sunrise, and the brass instruments flashed very brightly in the light. Of course the music was n't played at all on the Roman Catholic church, because the Roman Catholics did n't like Luther. There is a book which I read before I left America, called the Schönberg Cotta Family, and some parts of it you would like to read, I know. It tells about Luther when he was a poor little boy.

I went to a great German church yesterday. It was very large, and it looked larger because there were no galleries around it. The women sat by themselves, and the men by themselves. Besides the music of the organ, there was a band to play on their instruments, so that when all the people sung, the music was very loud, I can tell you. The German people sing much slower tunes than we do at home, and everybody sings. The hymns are not all read first by the minister, but the numbers of the hymns are printed in large figures, and placed around in different parts of the church, so that all can see them; and then when the organ commences to play, the people join in with the singing. I do n't like to go to a German church very well, because it does n't seem to be a very cheerful looking place, and I can't understand very well what is said; but I do like to hear the people sing, and see them sit so still in church. I think nobody turns around and gazes at other people as some Americans do at home.

Perhaps you would like to know what I did the rest of the day, Susie. I went to a Sunday School. Do n't you think I was happy? To be sure, it was a German school, and all the children were Germans; but it was so pleasant to think I was in a Sunday School once more. It made me think of my dear teacher at home.

Papa and an American gentleman (that I love very much) took me, and instead of going over the bridge, we went lower down and crossed the river in a little boat. Then we walked to a village, where a good gentleman has a Sunday School. An American gentleman was in Germany a few years ago, and told the people about the American Sunday Schools, and some of the people commenced having them here; but there is only one in Heidelberg. It did n't look like ours at home, and the teachers did n't teach just the same way that ours do. But they had little papers, and some of the stories and hymns are just like ours, because they are copied from our papers, and only changed into German. I heard them sing "I want to be an angel," in German, and I was so glad to hear that pretty tune again in a Sunday School.

Now I have finished my letter! I commenced by telling you how warm it was, and now I have just been writing about a Sunday School. I can't keep to one thing, Susie!

THIRTY-FIRST LETTER.

HEIDELBERG.

Dear Cousin Susie:

It is so nice to go up on the top of this house, to sit, in the evenings! The roof is flat, and very often just at sunset we take some cushions with us, and sit there till I have to go to bed. Then we can see the people in the streets, and the river, and the old Castle, and the sunset. I am in bed and asleep when the rest of the people in the house go to see the ruins by moonlight, and I do n't have any evening walks. But almost every morning after breakfast I have a walk with papa, and Caro follows us. We go to the post office first; not to see if there are any letters for us, because in this country all the letters are carried to the houses; but we buy stamps, or send letters to somebody very often. We send home to our friends a great many different kinds of stamps, but we hear that the American postmasters take them off. We have different money here to buy stamps and things with, from what we had in Bonn, and we have to pay a great many of these little kreutzers to get anything.

Oh, there are so many nice things to buy here! But mamma says, when we get to some great cities that we are going to, I shall see many prettier things that I want. Mamma does n't like to go shopping alone very well here in Germany, and it is n't very safe to send papa, for he makes such funny mistakes! I had something bought for me two days ago that I liked very much; that was, a sash of red, white and blue ribbon. The next day was Fourth of July, and we had n't any flag; so mamma said I might have a long sash to wear with my muslin dress. We could n't find a broad ribbon made of those three colors, and mamma bought narrow ribbon and sewed it together; so it looked just like one piece. It was the most quiet Fourth of July I ever saw, because of course the Germans did n't celebrate it, and the greatest pleasure I had was to wear my red, white and blue sash, and to go down stairs to visit William. His sisters are young ladies, but they are very kind to me, and they asked mamma if I might take tea with them. So I did, and they asked me to sing the Star Spangled Banner.

We did n't have any fire-works to see; but one evening lately we saw something about as pretty. I had gone to bed; but papa called me to get up, and we saw some boats filled with students sailing down the river, and every one had a great flaming torch, which lighted up his face, and they all together made the river and the shore light. They were singing merry songs, and every few minutes they threw up pretty colored balls — some like ours at fire-works — into the air, and then the sparks would fall upon the water, and it looked beautifully.

I ought to write to you a very good letter, to-day, Susie, because we are going away this week, probably, and I shall have so many new things to see, that I can't write any more about Heidelberg. I can't tell you about all my nice walks, because they have been so many. I haven't yet been tired once of looking at the old Castle, and every time I go there I find something which I hadn't seen before. Sometimes mamma and I go there to stay two or three hours; she reads, and I play with my dolls and make beds for them among the leaves. One day I carried my slate and pencil, and tried to draw a picture of a part of the Castle, as I had seen some ladies do; but it wasn't a very pretty picture, you would have thought.

I am very sorry we are going away so soon; but papa wishes to see some libraries in Gotha, and so we are going there. It is a very long way from here, and we shall go to Frankfort to stop a few days on the way, and perhaps some other places, too. Then I will write again. I am sorry we cannot stay here till the grapes are ripe, for this is the country for them, and I am afraid in Gotha we shall not find so many. But there is always something nice in every place, and so I will try and be happy.

I wish you were here to see this house, and this

pretty place, and our kind friends, before we go away. If you and Mary and Annie and little Walter were only with me all the time, how glad I should be! You don't know Walter, do you? He is the dearest little boy, and such a rogue!

Good bye, Susie, now! Don't forget that I send Aunt Susan a kiss in every letter I write. Sometimes I forget to speak of it, though.

Thirty-Second Letter.

FRANKFORT-ON-THE-MAIN.

Dear Susie:

It is raining so hard this afternoon that I must stay in-doors; and because my playthings are all packed up in the trunks, I have n't anything to do. I have looked out of the window and watched the people till I am tired, and so mamma has given me a sheet of paper and advised me to write to you. We have been here a day and a half, and have seen a number of pretty places and things, although it has rained almost all the time. When we came from Heidelberg in the cars, we had a terrible thunder shower; and the hail beat so against the windows that we were all frightened, and it has n't been pleasant since.

We stay in a hotel while we are in Frankfort. It is very amusing to see the different names on the hotels. Some are called the White Swan, the Green Tree, the Golden Ball, and some have no words painted at all, but only the sign of a gold fish, or a great crab, or something as funny. We walked around some, yesterday, and when we came near the great Cathedral, there were so many market women selling meat and fowls and vegetables and all kinds of fruit around it, that we could hardly get up to the door. But we at last went in, and saw the people having the same service that they did at Cologne. The church looked very old but it was n't very pretty; and after we had looked at the paintings we went to the top of the tower. Oh, dear, what a long journey it was to get there! And when we were at the very top, where it is so high that the people down in the streets look like little boys and girls, we found a little house there. I mean there were two or three rooms finished off, where a family lived who took care of the great bell. Would n't it seem strange to live in the top of such a high tower? It would be some like Jack's house on the bean-stalk, would n't it? When the people wanted water, a boy went down and fastened a pail full to some ropes which run on the outside, from this house to the ground, and they had a contrivance for drawing it up.

It made me think of London to walk through the streets yesterday; for there were so many people and carriages, and such beautiful stores. I thought some of the things I saw were much prettier than they were in London. There is one great street here which seems to have everything on it. It is called the Zeil. We went to some picture galleries, and to some sculpture galleries, and visited houses where distinguished men have lived, and saw pretty gardens and statues, and we thought that Frankfort would be a very fine place to live in. There were many soldiers in the streets who wore different kinds of uniforms. If you should walk through some of the streets, you would think Frankfort must be a very new city, because the streets are broad, and the houses so neat and beautiful. But there is a part which is very old, and there is one street which papa says every stranger visits, *because* it is so very old. I hardly ever saw such a disagreeable, strange-looking place; and we came upon it so suddenly, just after looking at handsome things, that, as mamma said, we seemed to be in another world. It is where the Jews live; and the street is called the Jews' street. It is very narrow, very narrow indeed; and the houses are so high and black, and so old looking, that it seemed as though they would really tumble over. The lower part of the houses were generally little shops, where people bought or sold things. We saw many old clothes hung up at the doors.

The men and women, and the children, too, had such a strange look. They did n't look as though they were good, and some of them were very dirty and ragged, as though they must be very poor. The men were trying to sell things, and were talking so loud that I thought they were quarrelling; and the women and children were sitting on the door-steps. Papa said if we walked through we could take our own time for looking at the houses, better than if we rode. He inquired which was the old Rothschild house, and

I think it was a better looking one than many of the others. You have heard what very rich men the Rothschilds are, have n't you? Only think, this old house used to be their home, and now they live in palaces! At one end of this dark, narrow street is the Jews' Synagogue, and it looked very new and pretty on the outside; but we could n't go into it.

I did n't know I had written so much! I hope you will like to read this letter, for I have liked to write it. It has made me forget the rainy weather. We are not going to be here much longer. After we have taken our long journey, I shall write again, and tell you how I enjoyed it.

Do n't forget me, Susie! I do n't forget you!

Thirty-Third Letter.

GOTHA.

Dear Cousin Susie:

I commenced a letter to you, telling about the home we have here; and then I remembered you had not heard anything about our journey to Frankfort. But there isn't much to tell about it, for it was a very warm day when we started, and I thought such a long ride was very tedious.

When we left Frankfort, early in the morning, we took the express train, and rode fast enough for three or four hours; then papa wanted to stop at a little city, to see a friend; and just by our waiting there for him to make a call, we lost the only express train there was before night. So we had to take the slow train, as it is called; that is, a long train of baggage cars, and a great many third-class cars; and it stops at every station on the road. But we had a good chance to see the country. We should have enjoyed it more if we could only have gone faster; for there was only one second-class car in the train, and we had it all to ourselves, and I lay down on the nice cushions and had a good nap. We rode on till six o'clock, then we were obliged to wait nearly two hours for another train. We had some supper, and took a walk to a little village about a mile away. You never saw such a place! Papa says that German villages are all alike; but this was the worst looking one I ever saw. Some of the houses were unpainted, and were surrounded by dirty yards, where the cows and pigs lived, and some were only whitewashed. I thought it was very strange, when I first came to Germany, to see all the beams of the houses in plain sight. In every German village you can see in every house the great beams running across each other; sometimes they are painted in a different color from the rest of the house, and sometimes not painted at all. The people in this little place gazed after us as though they had never seen any strangers before; but they were very polite, for the men all took off their hats, and the women spoke very civilly. Papa said, if we would like to we could spend the night, so that we could see the inside of a German inn in a village; but everything and everybody looked too untidy to tempt us much.

And yet we did have to spend the night in a village and in a little inn, although it was a little cleaner. We took the evening train, and papa thought we could at least get as far as Eisenach that night. Eisenach is a place which strangers visit, because there is an old castle there, where Martin Luther used to live. But we didn't get to Eisenach, for between eleven and twelve o'clock mamma woke me up, and said the cars had stopped and we could go no further. When we stepped upon the platform, we found we were near a little village, and must walk through the fields to get to a hotel or any place to sleep. There were some more people stopped with us, and though we were all tired and sleepy, we could n't help laughing, for the man who showed us the way with a lantern was so stupid that it seemed as though he did n't know what to do with us. At last we came to a small house, and went up some steep, narrow stairs to our rooms. The man left us a tallow candle to see by, and told us we had the best chambers in the house. We wondered what the worst could be, if ours were the best; for the floor was not very clean, and the table and chairs were so covered with dust that we could n't lay our things on them till we had wiped them with a towel. And oh, such beds! Have I ever told you about the German beds? They are always made narrow, for one person, and have a feather bed to sleep on instead of a mattrass, and generally a feather bed to sleep under, too, instead of a blanket or spread. In our nice homes along the Rhine we have always had sheets, and generally a coverlet, instead of a thick feather bed, to cover us with; but in this house I am telling you about, we had no sheets and no white cases to the beds either. Each of our beds was made up in the same way, with a thick, soft feather bed, covered with pink calico, to sleep on, and another like it to put over us. How would you like such a bed in a hot July night? I know we did n't sleep much!

For breakfast we had some miserable coffee and some hard, dry bread, and then we were glad to leave such a funny place, and take the morning train for Gotha. I think I shall like Gotha; it seems to be a pretty little city, and if we get a pleasant home, I shall have a great many things to write to you about. We could n't find any rooms to be let, and papa was almost discouraged looking for them. At last we heard of this place, and we shall go away as soon as we can get a better one. We are on a pretty street, but we have to go through such a dark entry and up such a bad staircase; and there is a soap shop below, so we are smelling soap all the time in these hot days.

I wish I knew what you are doing now! Are you writing a letter to me?

Thirty-Fourth Letter.

GOTHA.

Dear Cousin Susie:

I wish you could see how pretty Gotha is! It hasn't any great river Rhine, like Bonn, nor any beautiful old castle, like Heidelberg; but all around the city are handsome houses, and great gardens and parks. Perhaps you will think, because I said there was no beautiful old castle here, that there isn't any; but there is. It is an immense building on a hill, but the walls are not broken down like those at Heidelberg, and it isn't pretty, either. I can't tell you a great deal about the town itself, for it seems very much like the other places in Germany that I have written about; only I think it is the neatest, cleanest city I have seen. There are no walls and gates, and no trees. The streets are very narrow, but have better sidewalks than in Bonn, because there they were so narrow that only one person could walk along nicely. The houses are packed closely together, and have no blinds; and they look so hot this summer weather. The gutters at the side of the street are covered over with boards; they are not filled with dirty water, because clean water is forced into them, and is all the time running through them. When I am walking along, I often see the servant girls lifting up a loose board and dipping their pails into the water. The people don't drink this water, but I suppose it is clean enough to wash floors and stairs with.

You would laugh if you could see the peasant women here, and the funny way they dress. They don't wear white handkerchiefs on their heads, as did those of Bonn, but the strangest looking bonnets and head dresses! When they come into market with fruit and vegetables, they have a kind of old-fashioned bonnet, with a band of black ribbon over it, perched on the top of their heads; but Sundays, and when they seem to be dressed up a little, they wear a kind of — I don't really know what to call it — turban, or something, made of black satin ribbon. Some black silk is bound around the head, something like a turban, and on the top of it are placed several enormous bows of ribbon, with wire in them, so they will stand up straight, and then streamers of ribbon, two or three yards long, hang down the back. They wear them to church, and seem to think they are as pretty as you and I do a new hat. That makes me think, Susie, do you wear the same hat you did last summer? I see all kinds of hats here, and all kinds of dresses, though the German ladies dress very much like the American ladies, mamma says.

It seems so strange to see women work so hard as they do in Germany. Whenever we have rode through the country the poor women have been digging in the fields, or ploughing, or sawing wood, and their little children would be helping them. Once we saw a mother at work digging, and her little baby was asleep in a cradle near her, out in the fields.

Very often, here in Gotha, I see women harnessed into carts, and drawing great loads, as though they were horses. Sometimes a dog or donkey will be fastened in with them, for they make the dogs work very hard. Every day little carts, and sometimes great ones, go past our house, full of milk, or vegetables, or bags of meal, and poor dogs have to draw them, and a little boy or girl walks along by the side to drive the dogs and to help unload the things when they get to market. I pity the poor peasant women so much! They don't carry their baskets of wood and vegetables on their heads, as the Bonn women did, but on their backs; and though they look so stout and strong, sometimes they are bent almost double by having such a heavy load. There are two leather straps fastened to their baskets, and they slip their arms through these, and then walk sometimes many miles. Every Wednesday and Saturday they come in from the country to the markets here, and then mamma and I have a chance to get nice fruit; and our landlady gets our fresh butter and eggs then, too. The only trouble we have in going to buy anything is, the peasants speak such bad German we can hardly understand them. There are no Americans in Gotha, and only a few English people, so we don't hear much but German; but it is so hard to learn to speak it that I can't say many sentences yet. If I go to a Kindergarden, perhaps I shall learn faster.

The shops here are not very nice. I almost think the butcher shops are the best of all. You will laugh at that, but the butcher shops are very different from ours. They are as neat as your sitting room, and the meat is either laid on marble shelves, or hung up on pretty hooks. They sell a great many sausages here, (papa says the Gotha sausage is famous,) and they are hung in rows in the windows. I like to eat the sausages, but I cannot swallow the black bread, it is so sour.

THIRTY-FIFTH LETTER.

GOTHA.

Dear Susie:

I am sitting on a beautiful balcony to write this letter. I must tell you how we happened to come to such a pretty place. Do you remember I told you that we had not a pleasant home here in Gotha? Papa made inquiries for rooms, but he couldn't find any until he had advertised in the papers, and then he found this place where we are now. I am so glad we came here, for we have such a pleasant, kind landlady, (though she is a very old lady,) and she has such a good-natured servant. We have a pretty sitting room, and then, best of all, we have this great balcony, as large as a room, which leads off from the sitting room. I have so much room now, that mamma says there will be no excuse for me if she finds my books and dolls' clothes out of order; and I have a little bureau to keep my things in.

The furniture in our rooms is very old-fashioned: the sofa has such a prim-looking back and arms, and the great arm chairs look so dignified that I am almost afraid to sit in one; but they are pretty, too, for the seats and backs are beautifully embroidered with worsted roses and leaves. The old lady we live with says her daughters used to do such work many years ago, and she told us the three portraits on the wall were her three daughters. Whenever I glance up at them their eyes seem to be looking right at me, and follow me everywhere about the room. Is n't it strange that the eyes of a portrait follow us so? We have a number of nice tables, and pretty little seats, and a large writing desk in our sitting room; and in one corner is a white porcelain stove. It rests on the floor and reaches almost to the top of the room. There are four sides to it; and on the front side and the top are pretty figures made out of porcelain. There are two little bright brass doors, too, and I almost wish cold weather would come, so that I could see if it warms the room like our stoves at home. Papa says it takes a long time to heat up such a stove, but it keeps the heat a long time.

On one side of our room is a pretty arch of lattice work, covered with green ivy; and when we wish to go on the balcony we open a glass door under this arch. Oh, it is the very nicest place out here! It seems like a kind of room out of doors; for there is a little fence all around it, so no one can fall down, (it is one story up from the street,) and there are white settees and tables in it, where we can sit and read or sew, or have our tea. There is no roof, but a great tree hangs over it, and shades it from the sun. Every morning I bring my playthings out here, and play; and if I am tired of them, there is enough for me to see around me. The Duke's palace is very near us, just across the street, and beautiful houses and gardens all around us. Our house is on one side of a square, so we can see the streets on both sides of us, and in front, too. It is much pleasanter being a little way out of the city, as we are now, for the houses are better, and the trees and gardens much prettier.

I like very much to watch the people and carriages going by. The street on one side of us leads to the depôt, so that all day long people are going and coming. There are some people who ride along in splendid carriages, and perhaps just after or before them will be a cart drawn by donkeys, and a woman or a boy driving them. But Sunday is the time to see the people pass; and it seems all day as though it must be some great holiday. Just as soon as I look out of the windows in the morning, I see men and women and children hurrying past to take the train. They are all dressed in their best clothes, and are going to some favorite place to spend the day. And the peasant men and women come crowding into the city, to go to church, or to walk in the parks, or to go to the beer gardens. The little boys and girls who come from the country are dressed like old men and women, but they do n't seem to think so.

I have just been stopping for a few minutes to see

the guards changed at the palace. You would n't think .such a plain looking house could be called a palace, but the Duke lives here in the winters, and so soldiers stand before it all day and night. Once in two hours new ones come from the castle, and the others go away. I like to hear the officers give the loud commands to them. But instead of looking at them, I ought to have been writing my letter to you.

Can you read my writing easily, Susie?

THIRTY-SIXTH LETTER.

GOTHA.

Dear Susie:

I want to tell you where we went to church yesterday. The Sunday before we attended the church in the old palace on the hill. It is called the Royal Church, because the Duke and his court attend it when they are in Gotha. I suppose you don't know that this Duke I write about is the brother-in-law of Queen Victoria. Prince Albert, who died, was his own brother. I didn't know it till papa told me. That church was very handsome in the inside; there were beautiful pictures and carving, and the pulpit for the minister was splendid, and the music was very pretty; but as the service was in German, of course I couldn't understand very well many things. It seems very different in a German church from an American church; you know in America the people can sit in any part of the house they wish, if they only pay for their seats; but in this country the seats are all free, and people can sit anywhere if they only sit with their own class. I mean, that the Duke and his friends have a certain part given to them, and they have velvet cushioned chairs to sit on; and the very rich people, and those who hold some high office, have a certain place for them to sit. Their seats are generally in the gallery, and the rest of the congregation sit below where they please; only mamma and I noticed that the peasant women and girls with their long black streamers sat a good way back; and the servant girls, too, who wear nothing on their heads. Would n't it look funny in America to see women come in to a meeting without any kind of a bonnet on their heads? I have seen hundreds do só in Germany.

But I had quite forgotten that I was going to tell you about the Moravian church, which we went to yesterday. It was a few miles away, and when we reached the little village where the Moravians live, it seemed as though it was the first quiet place we had seen on Sabbath day in Germany. The streets were all still, for the stores were closed, and the people were in their houses. We went to the little church, which looked almost like a plain house, and waited till the people came; but it was not long, for the service commenced early. I did wish you were with me, for you would have seen what you never did before! The men and boys came, dressed in black, all of them, and went in at one door, and sat by themselves; and the ladies and girls sat by themselves. The ladies all wore plain looking dresses and capes, and on their heads they wore little white muslin or lace caps, just alike.

The only difference about these caps was, they were tied and trimmed with different colors of ribbon. If they were widows, they wore white; if they were married, they wore blue; and the others wore a deep shade of pink. The young ladies and little girls were dressed in the same manner, only their caps were trimmed with light pink ribbon. They all went into church in procession, and sat by themselves in seats before the minister. I sat with mamma at one side, and I did n't see one of them turn around to look at the others, but when they were not singing they kept their hands folded, and were perfectly still. I hardly dared to move; and once when I sneezed, I was almost afraid I should be sent out. I can't tell you what the minister said, but he seemed to preach as though he wanted to do the people good. The singing was beautiful, and everybody sung. The strangers have seats at the side of the church, and the peasant women sit there, too. Two of them sat by me, and their dress looked as strangely as that of the Moravian ladies.

When church was over, all went out in procession, and then we walked into the burying ground behind the church. It was a very pretty, quiet spot, but it was very unlike our cemeteries at home. The grave stones, instead of standing at the head of the graves, were in the form of a cross sometimes, and were always lying on the top of the grave mound. The men and women were each buried by themselves, in long rows, one after the other; and the one who was buried last came at the end of the long row. The little children were by themselves; and on their grave stones were such pretty German words, which did n't say they had died, but had fallen asleep, or had gone home. Papa says there are some excellent christian people among the Moravians, and I should like to go to their church again.

Can you understand at all what a pleasant day we had, from what I have written?

I am going to a Kindergarten in two or three days.

Thirty-Seventh Letter.

GOTHA.

Dear Susie:

I go to the Kindergarten every day, but I wish I could say I liked to go. If it was only in America, and there was an American teacher and scholars, it would be much pleasanter for me. But I am learning fast to speak German, so that perhaps in a week or two I shall enjoy more going to this school. There are a great many little children there, and some are almost babies; for they are allowed to enter the Kindergarten when they are only three years old. Then there are a few boys and girls as large as I am. We have great rooms to stay in, and we do n't have to study at all. I thought it was very nice, the first few days, to play so much; but now I am a little tired of the same things over and over. There are a great many teachers, and they try to think of different games for us, and different things to make; but we generally know what will come for each day of the week. When we go in the morning, for a long time the whole school stay together, and we have games and marches and songs; some of them are so funny they would make you laugh. The little children hop around as though they were rabbits. After we have played a while together we divide; the great ones go into one room by themselves, and the little ones into another. Then we sit at little tables, and sometimes make block houses, like what the teacher makes for us, and sometimes we draw, or make pretty things from paper or willow. I wish you could see the show-case full of pretty things which the children have made. The principal teacher has a room, where he teaches young ladies to make and do the same things which we do, so that they will learn to be teachers. I generally go home alone at noon, and I do n't go again in the afternoon.

I like to watch the funny-looking people that I see in the street; and it always makes me laugh to see the way people have their wood sawed here in Gotha. Instead of having one man to saw a load of wood and take his own time for it, a dozen men, and women, too, are hired all at once to work together, and they work sawing and splitting at the sides of the streets. Just think what a little time it must take to finish a load of wood! And when they have finished one job, they march in procession to another place, and commence working again. One day last week mamma and I counted over twenty men in our garden sawing wood, and women were helping them. A man takes hold of one end of the saw, and a woman the other end; and they work all day, only when they stop at noon to drink their beer and eat their bread and sausage.

We have beautiful places to walk in here. I believe

I have not told you about the great parks, have I? They belong to the Duke, and are full of beautiful paths, and trees, and little ponds. On every path are pretty white seats, and sometimes mamma and I go and sit on one for two or three hours; she carries a book, and I take my doll or slate. One day I tried to write a composition on my slate, but it was rather a funny thing. I like much better to write a letter. These parks are so large that we can walk for hours; and when we wish to go home, we very often go through the orange gardens. These are full of the most beautiful flowers, of all the kinds I ever saw, and there are hundreds of orange and lemon trees. I cannot tell you how sweet the air is, nor how pleasant it is to walk through this place, or to sit on one of the white settees and look at the flowers. The German children have to be very careful not to touch anything so as to injure it, and they are not allowed in some of the parks without a nurse or older person to watch them.

Yesterday two little girls came to play with me on my balcony. They had never seen an American doll before, although there are a great many china dolls here. We had a nice play, and next week I am going to visit them. They have a rocking-horse, and a seesaw, and all kinds of playthings. I wonder if you keep all your playthings as nicely as you used to, on that broad shelf in the sitting room! It always made me think of a little store.

Thirty-Eighth Letter..

SCHNEPFENTHAL.

Dear Susie:

You see I am not in Gotha to-day, but this place is only seven miles away, and we are going back there again in a few days. Perhaps you will laugh at me, and think that I always call the last place I visit the prettiest one of all I have seen; but certainly I do think we haven't seen such a pretty place since we left America. Schnepfenthal is only a little village, but it is a charming one, for it is on a hill, and in the middle of all the houses is the great white building called the Institute, where boys attend school. The boys all dress alike, and wear bright red jackets; and when they are out of school and playing on the green grass, you can't think what a pretty sight it is!. It seems like a picture. But the most beautiful place, and the one that strangers go to visit, is about a mile beyond Schnepfenthal, and called Reinhardtsbrunnen. It is where the Duke's country palace is, and papa says he couldn't have chosen a more lovely spot. The palace itself is very pretty; it used to be an old nunnery, but the Duke had it all made over and altered, only he had preserved just enough of the old form in some parts, to have us see what a strange looking house must have been there. At one end is such a beautiful chapel, and the ivy and woodbine twine over it, and over the palace windows, too. All around are the most lovely gardens and beds of pretty flowers, and great trees and a succession of ponds. One is just before the palace, and they reach on, one after the other, almost to Schnepfenthal. On the ponds are pretty boats, and through the gardens are walks and fountains and more of the white seats where people can rest. When the Duke is not in Reinhardsbrunnen, people are allowed to walk up to the very palace and through the court-yard and peep into the Duke's private garden. Papa calls this place a paradise, and it does seem like one, for all around on every side are hills and mountains, and covered to the top with trees, and taken such care of that they have wide, smooth walks across them and through them. The Duke owns all these woods, and he spends the summer months in hunting with his friends in them. I think these woods reach as far as Friedrichroda, a little town a mile beyond, for I know we walked through the trees all the way there, instead of going in the road. There is one hotel near the palace, and that and all the hotels in Friedrichroda are full of strangers, because so many come here to see these beautiful places.

We can't come from Gotha to this place in the cars

without changing cars and then walking some, so we came in a post-wagon. But the time we came here before, about three weeks ago, (did I ever tell you about that?) we rode on the top of an omnibus. It was such a funny ride! but I enjoyed it, for we had a good chance to see people as we rode along. I saw women and girls digging in the fields, and boys coming from some village with a wheel-barrow full of loaves of black bread, and men drinking beer at the little inns we passed, and more of such amusing sights.

We didn't stay long that time, and when we went back to Gotha we became acquainted with a lady who was in the omnibus with us; and we learned to love her so much after we went to our home, that we accepted her invitation to come here again. Her friends live in Schnepfenthal, and teach in the Institute.

The way we became acquainted with this lady was rather strange. It was in the evening, and I was tired, because we had walked so much that day, and I wanted to go to sleep. Mamma kept telling me stories to keep me awake, and she supposed all the people in the omnibus were Germans and could not understand us. But bye and bye this lady spoke to me and said, "See the moon!" and then we knew she could speak English. After that we met her very often in the parks, and we became well acquainted with her, and she is one of the best friends we have in Gotha. She came here with us this time, and it is her friends that we see here, and whom we visit, although we do not live at their house.

I did mean to tell you what a funny place we were living in here, but I must keep that for the next time. I do n't say nearly all I want to in any letter.

Thirty-Ninth Letter.

SCHNEPFENTHAL.

Dear Susie:

Every time I want to write this long word, I have to ask papa to spell it for me. He just told me that it means Snipe's valley, in English; and that Reinhardtsbrunnen is Foxes' well. You wouldn't think from their names that they were such pretty places, would you? Didn't I say in my last letter I would tell you what kind of a place we lived in here? You would have to guess a good many times before you guess right. But first I want to tell you how we came from Gotha to Schnepfenthal.

Because it is so late in the season now, (you know we have been in Gotha some weeks,) the omnibuses do not run any longer, and we had to go to the Gotha post office and engage seats in the post-wagon, which comes here once a day. It was the funniest kind of carriage that I ever rode in. It was something like a square box, about a quarter as large as an omnibus, and set on high wheels; on the top of it was a seat for the driver and post-man, and under it a smaller box to hold the letters. We stepped into the wagon by a little door in the rear, and found seats for six people. The driver carries a brass horn, and whenever he goes near a village or town he plays a tune upon it; it sounds very prettily, we thought. I was very glad when we were really here. We went to our friends in Schnepfenthal to see where they had secured rooms for us, because we knew all the hotels were full.

And now I'll tell you, Susie; we live in a mill! But it isn't anything like any mill you ever saw, for it looks on the outside like a very nice large house, all neat and painted. In one part of it is a little mill, but two-thirds of the building are fitted up into beautiful rooms, which are let to strangers in the summer time. I said there was one house, but there are two very near together. When we leave the street we go through a great yard,— where I always see some hens and a black dog, and sometimes the mill door is open and I see bags of meal,— and then into the part of the house where we live. Our rooms are up stairs, and so pleasant! The sitting room is as neat as wax, and from the windows we can look one way and see Schnepfenthal, and the other way is Reinhardtsbrunnen; for we are about half way between them, and our house is in the middle of green fields. But the place is called the Mill.

There are two girls that are daughters of one of our dear, good Schnepfenthal friends, that I like very much; and though they are both older than I am, we have nice plays together. Eliza, the oldest one, can speak English pretty well, but Lenchen only talks in German or French, and so we do n't say much to each other. Sunday morning they came to our house with their aunt, and wanted us to go to church with them. It was such a pretty little church: in the same building where the Institute is. There was a little gallery, where the ladies and strangers sat, and below were the teachers and the scholars. The boys wore those jackets I wrote about, and sat very still till the service was over; but when they were once out on the green they made noise enough.

Besides the church, there are school-rooms, and great halls full of curiosities, and stuffed birds and animals, and a large public parlor and dining room, and the rooms where the Principal's family live, and many rooms of course for the boys to study and sleep in, all in one building. The parlor was very pretty, for it was full of beautiful presents, which former pupils had sent to their teachers; and the four sides of the room were really covered with little portraits of the boys. The dining room was very pleasant, too, and everything was in perfect order.

You know, Susie, that the Germans do not keep Sunday as we do, and they think it right to work and play if they wish to. The boys on the common were having games when we went out, and the ladies of the family that we took dinner with had their sewing and knitting in their hands. Eliza's father lent me a book in English to read; but I am afraid that I shall have no time to read it, for to-morrow, if it is pleasant, we are all going to the top of a high mountain, called the Spiesberg.

I like the German people very much. There are a great many things I see that seem so funny I want to laugh; but yet some of the people we meet are so very kind and good, I cannot help loving them. I hope some time you will come to Schnepfenthal and see this dear good family we love so much. The sister that I told you lives in Gotha, came here with us in the post-wagon. Every day when we are in Gotha we walk in the park with her, and she speaks English with us, and we speak German with her.

It is pretty late now. Mamma says I must go to bed early to-night, because we shall walk so much to-morrow. So good night, my dear cousin Susie!

FORTIETH LETTER.

SCHNEPFENTHAL.

My dear Susie:

I shall have to write very fast this morning, because we are going back to Gotha as soon as the post-wagon comes past. I am very much disappointed that we cannot stay here longer; but the pleasant warm weather seems to have gone, for to-day it is cold and very rainy. We could not go out to walk if we stayed.

We had such a nice time yesterday! A party of us started at nine o'clock for a long walk, the longest I ever took. We all wore thick boots and warm travelling dresses, (I always wear my Scotch wincey when we go on such an excursion,) and a servant girl went with us to help carry the thick shawls, and she had a great basket strapped on her back full of bread and meat and dishes, and things we might want. It was a lovely morning to start, for the sun was shining so brightly that the whole country looked most beautiful. We went on through woods and green fields, and up little hills, but all the way was a good path.

Sometimes we would meet peasant men or women, bare-footed, and having great loads on their backs; and they would always salute us and say, "Guten Tag," which means "good day" in English.

Lenchen and I trudged on in front of the rest, and picked pretty grasses, or played with our stout canes that papa cut for us off the trees; but we hardly spoke a word together all the way, for I was afraid to speak much German, and she was too shy to say anything. Mamma thought she looked very much like you, Susie, she said so a number of times. We kept on and on, till at last I was so tired I had to sit down on a stone, and so one of the ladies said, that as we were two-thirds of the way up, we would all rest and have something to eat. So papa chose a nice place under the trees, and spread the shawls, and we all sat down on the ground. The servant girl took off her basket, — I pitied her, she looked so tired, — and the plates were passed around, and one of the ladies cut the meat and spread the bread and butter. It seemed as though nothing ever tasted so good as that did. While we were sitting there we could hear the deer crying in the woods around us, and once we saw one. Mamma says I mustn't say they cried, but bellowed. The woods here in Germany look differently from ours in America, because the trees are standing in regular rows. Papa told me why they looked so. Every thirty years the old forests are cut down, and new ones are planted, and the little trees are set in rows.

so that when they are grown large they looked as I saw them.

After we rested awhile we went a little further, and then came out on the top of a mountain not as high as the Spiesberg, but yet we had a beautiful prospect all around us. We were surrounded by hills, and between them in the valleys were villages with red-roofed houses; and close by us was a strange looking house where the Duke rested with his friends when he was hunting. As we went through the woods we saw a party of German men chopping wood, and they spoke such funny German I could n't understand anything they said. Lenchen and I saw the top of the Spiesberg first. There is a little house there for people to rest in, and people live in it and provide coffee or beer for anybody who wishes it. Our party went up stairs into a little room and stayed several hours. Some of the ladies had their knitting work, and some talked, and Eliza and Lenchen played with me until I fell asleep. When I woke, some more friends had come, and then we had such a nice dinner. We had cold meat, and brown bread and white bread, and butter and cheese, and coffee and beer, and pears and plums, and some grapes that had come all the way from Switzerland. Oh, they were so delicious that they seemed to melt in my mouth! We were very much disappointed in one thing, for very soon after we reached the top, all the clear sky was covered with clouds, and we could n't see much but mist. I had rather a bad fall when we went down. It was not the same way we went up. I suppose I ran too fast; for down I went on my knees, and then I had to limp all the way home; and this morning I am a little lame.

Don't you think we had a nice time? When we left Boston I could not walk one quarter as far as I can now, without being all tired out. I suppose now it is time for me to put on my hat and sacque, and be ready to go.

Forty-First Letter.

GOTHA.

Dear Susie:

I do n't know how many letters I have written to you from Gotha, but I want to send one more before we leave this nice pleasant home of ours. But I am not writing to-day on the balcony, for it is too cold. The glass door is shut, and we have a fire in our porcelain stove, and my table is moved up near it.

Yesterday I went with our servant girl to the market, and she brought home a basket of wood on her back. She wears a funny kind of cape or cloak when she goes out, made of brown calico, and it is trimmed with two broad full ruffles, and she never has a bonnet on her head. She is so kind to me that I am very sorry to leave her, and she wants to go to America with us. She is very honest, too, and German servants are not always so. The ladies who keep house always carry a bunch of keys around with them, and keep everything locked up,—even sugar, and butter, and such things. Mamma says, perhaps if servants were more trusted they would n't be so sly and dishonest.

We have such a dear good landlady! We had often heard that German landladies would take advantage of people, and sometimes cheat them; but this one of ours is as kind as she can be. She does n't work any herself, but is able to totter around on her cane, and see if things are in order. Every day when I go to the hotel to dinner, or while I am in the Kindergarten, she comes into our room and leaves some fruit or cake on the table; and sometimes she allows me to water her plants on the balcony. After tea she likes to have me go into her room and sing some little English song; and I try to help her down the stairs when she goes to church on Sundays. She has a little carriage which she is pushed along in. We do n't go very often to the church which she attends.

And that makes me think, Susie, I want to tell you about one old, strange-looking church here in Gotha. When we went there first, and walked through a grave-yard towards it, I could hardly believe but it was a great house. But the inside is the strangest. It is not painted at all, and the seats are of plain boards, without any cushions, or else they are old-fashioned chairs of different kinds. The pulpit is small and high, and has a table before it, with a cross and two candles upon it. There are no blinds nor curtains to the windows, and a gallery runs around, where young people sit. In one part are the soldiers, too, and just opposite the pulpit is the band of singers, who sing and play on brass instruments when the hymns are given out. But though this old church looks so differently from all the others here in Gotha—because they have splendid paintings and rich carving—yet there is something else which I have n't yet told you, which interested us the most of anything. All around on the front of the gallery are hung wreaths of dried or artificial flowers tied with ribbons; and between them are portraits of children, though I think there are two or three of older people. These wreaths used to be laid on the coffins of those who had died, and after they were buried, their friends brought the wreaths into this old church, and hung them up. Sometimes they are in frames, and some are laid in glass boxes. The portraits are of little children who have died, and their friends can't forget them, because every time they go to meeting they see those pictures.

There are two or three cemeteries beyond the one where the church is, and we sometimes walk through them. All the grave stones are in the form of crosses, and on nearly all the graves there are wreaths lying. We saw the ivy growing all over Mr. Perthes' grave. Did you ever hear about Mr. Frederick Perthes? He was a very good German man, and had an excellent wife, and a book has been written about them in German and English. Their sons and daughters live in Gotha, and papa goes to their houses.

Papa and mamma go often to a great many places where I can't go, and I can't tell you about them, because I don't see for myself. There have been some very nice concerts which I have not heard, and there has been a great fair or something of that kind, which I have not seen. I didn't want to go, for I was afraid of the noise of the guns. Mamma went, and she saw all kinds of playthings, and all kinds of cakes, and all kinds of people, I should think, from what she said.

Yesterday I saw Prince Alfred at the palace here. He is Queen Victoria's son, and is going to be the next Duke here. He was standing at his chamber window, and I wanted to sing "God save the Queen," but I didn't know the words. He looks like a nice young man.

Perhaps this will be my last letter from Gotha.

Forty-Second Letter.

ERFURT.

Dear Cousin Susie:

Last night I was in my little bed in Gotha, and tonight we are in a great hotel. The reason I write so soon again is, because I am afraid I shall forget some of the things I want to say, if I do n't tell them now.

I entirely forgot to write anything about the old palace in Gotha, and now it is too late. I can just tell you something about the size of it, or rather what is in it, and then you can judge what a great building it must be. Besides the great church which is in one corner of it, there are great libraries, and halls full of collections of coins, and of animals and birds, and galleries of paintings and statues, and apartments where princes' families live, and offices, and splendid halls fitted up for the Duke to live in if he wishes to, and rooms without number for his servants. Would n't you think it must be large?

Papa says if we should ever visit Gotha again, he thinks we should not see our dear good landlady, for she is so very old and feeble now. Whenever we spoke to her we called her Mrs-Councilloress Henniberg, because her husband used to be a councillor, and she is always addressed by his title. That is always the case here in Germany, I am told.

We are in a great hotel, just opposite the depôt; and are in a great room, too. We are all sitting around a great table in one corner, and mamma and I are are on the sofa beside it, and papa in a great chair. Just before we began to write, (for we are all writing,) a servant brought us some tea, and some gingerbread to eat with it. We had a pretty silver teapot (it looked like silver) and a little strainer to pour the tea through. The tea was weak enough, but I liked that, because I could have a little. Here in Germany the children drink sugar-water; that is, a glass of water with sugar dissolved in it.

We have been walking about ever since we came here. I should n't like to live in Erfurt, for it seems to be such a very old city. There are walls and fortifications around it, and the streets are very narrow, and really no sidewalks at all; or if any, they are just wide enough for me alone. We went into a store and bought some pretty pictures as we walked along, and then we went to Luther's cell. You know Martin Luther was a monk, once, and he used to live and study in a convent at Erfurt. It is n't a convent any longer, but is now a school for orphans; but the cell of Martin Luther has been preserved just as it used to be when he was in it. As we went through the yard we saw a great many orphan boys gazing at us, and a woman came up to us to show us the way. We went up a flight of stairs into an old building and through a very long hall. You would never forget that long hall, Susie, if you should once see it; for on both sides it is covered with great pictures, called the Dance of Death, papa told me. Every picture was in a frame, and was different from the one next to it; but in every one was the figure of Death appearing like a horrible skeleton, and just ready to seize the people in the painting. None of the people seemed to know that Death was so near them, for some were reading, or writing, or laughing, or dancing, or dressing for parties; and yet he was just behind them. There were pictures of children, too, and dear little babies who were playing so happily; but he was coming up to take them away from their mothers who were bending over them, but who couldn't see him. There were men and women of all ages, and doing all kinds of work, but that terrible skeleton was always near them.

When we went into the cell, the door was so low that papa had to stoop. It was a little room, with one small window in it; and Luther's chair, and his table, and his inkstand. In a glass case were some old books, but they were not his. A great portrait of him hung against the wall, and he looked like a large stout man. I have heard much more about Luther since we came to Germany than I ever knew before, and I was very glad to see things of his, though I don't think I cared as much about it as papa and mamma did.

There is a great cathedral in Erfurt, and we went to see it. It is very beautiful in the inside. The windows are of stained glass, and there are fine paintings, and some of the nicest wood carving we have seen. There was some tapestry, too, hanging against the wall, hundreds of years old. When we went out, papa had no small pieces of money in his pocket, and he had to give our guide twice the usual fee; but she did not even say "Thank you." If we had waited till to-morrow morning we could have seen it in service time and paid nothing, for the Roman Catholics have a service every morning.

I am so tired I must go to bed now. My great feather bed in the corner is waiting for me.

FORTY-THIRD LETTER.

LEIPZIG.

DEAR SUSIE:

You will get letters pretty often from me, until we get to Berlin, for, as I wrote to you day before yesterday in my Erfurt letter, if I do n't say at once what I have in my thoughts, I shall forget some of it. I cannot tell you much about anything in this city, excepting about the great fair. Every fall there are great sales here of all kinds of things, and people come from great distances to see and buy. The hotels and even all the lodging houses are full of strangers, and papa had no easy time to find us nice rooms. The streets are crowded with people. It makes me think of London every time I go out; for I am pushed off the sidewalk into the street, and then back again. The shop windows are full of the most beautiful things, and we have been so many weeks in that little quiet Gotha, that I am really glad to see so many pretty things again.

I cannot give you any idea what crowds of people there are here, nor how full the streets are of booths. These booths are made like little houses with one side open, and a counter or broad shelf built up, covered with things to sell. You can hardly think of any kind of a thing that anybody could want, that is n't to be found in plain sight. Some booths are full of cakes and gingerbread, and when anybody passes, the woman who is behind the shelf calls out, "Buy! buy! buy!" Perhaps the next person will have china and glass ware to sell, and so on. There is everything. Boots, and stockings, and collars, and dolls, and every kind of plaything, and fruit, and table linen, and iron, and, oh, Susie, I get tired even thinking of all I saw! Some of the things are very cheap, and I bought a little box and vase, and some more little things, for only one groschen apiece. Papa was standing at one table where there were photographs, and when he paid for those he bought, he probably drew out a package of money from his pocket, and it fell on the ground; for after a while he found it was gone. We went back to the same place, but somebody must have taken it, because papa never found it. I was very sorry, because he was going to buy some pretty things in Leipzig, and now he can't. Is n't it too bad?

Leipzig is much larger now than it was some time ago, papa tells me. Around the old city used to be a wall, but now it is taken down, and where it used to be is a broad, beautiful walk, called the Promenade. Mamma and I walked around it yesterday afternoon; we were sure we could not be lost, for as it is a circle we knew we should come back to the place we started from. There are nice seats for people to rest, and rows of trees the whole way; and then on one side of us was the old city, with the houses built very closely together, and on the other side were pretty streets and handsome houses and fine gardens. As mamma and I walked along, we would meet little children and their nurses; and women selling apples or pears; and the city people idling along. Once we saw a whole orphan school going by in procession. Sometimes we would pass a large square, where there were tents with shows, and booths full of toys, and swings for children. There was one nice contrivance for boys and girls that I never saw before. I wish I could describe it so you could understand what it was. It was something like a great wheel, I should think, not standing, but as though it was flat, only raised a few feet from the ground. The hub was a high pole, and at the end of each spoke was a little kind of carriage, with sometimes a seat for two and sometimes for four children, and there were imitation horses attached to it. After the girls and boys had taken their seats in the different carriages, the machine which made them turn would begin to move, and the band of music would play, and then the children would go round and round, and faster and faster. Mamma thought I should be dizzy, so I did n't have any ride.

It seems as though I had n't written much in this letter, but a gentleman has just come in, and I can't write when people are talking.

Forty-Fourth Letter.

DRESDEN.

Dear Susie:

We came here yesterday, and had a most delightful ride. The weather was so warm that we had the car windows open all the way, and the country was so pretty that it was a pleasure for all of us to look at it. There were a great many peasant women and children working in the fields, and sometimes it seemed as though they were their homes; for there was often no house to be seen, and the whole family would be together. The baby was in such a funny kind of cradle, and one of the larger children was making a fire under a black iron pot to cook the dinner; and one family we saw were resting from work and were sitting on the ground, eating a lunch.

About an hour before we came in sight of Dresden, we saw beautiful hills and vineyards. It seemed really as though on the left side of us, there was a succession of hills; and on the top of each one was a splendid house, and at the bottom was a little village.

I suppose I shall not write you the same things

about Dresden that gentlemen and ladies write, for a great many places that papa and mamma visit, I do not see. This morning we started to visit the Picture Gallery, (do you know this is called almost the finest gallery in the world?) but papa found it was being cleaned, and was only open to visitors for a few hours, and he must pay quite a fee; so, as he thought I should not enjoy it very much, and I had seen so many large galleries in London, he left me at a nice place, where he was going to get our dinner. Our hotel was too far away for me to go back to it, and papa found this nice eating house, where I had a sofa and table all to myself, and a large black dog to play with.

After we had taken dinner, (I had some pudding that tasted like an American pudding,) we walked around to see the splendid churches, and the old palace, and the great theatre, and the markets and streets. The shop windows are full of pictures, and of other pretty things, also. I don't see so many book-stores here as I did in Leipzig, for it seemed there as though every other shop was a book-seller's. The people in Leipzig must be great readers, I should think.

When we were walking through one of the market places this afternoon, we saw, besides the pears and apples and grapes,—oh, such delicious grapes they were, too!—some ripe tomatoes. We had n't seen any before this summer, and I was perfectly delighted and I think papa was as much so as I was. You know we eat them raw in America if we wish to; and papa likes them so very much, but the Germans never heard of such a thing, and only use them cooked in soups. Papa knew this and he thought we would give the woman who sold them, a surprise; so he asked her what those red things were as though he had never seen them before, and put one to his mouth as if he would taste it. "Oh my noble sir, they are not made to eat so! do not taste it, noble sir, before it is cooked!" But papa only smiled, and gave one to me and one to mamma, and we all ate them as though they were oranges. The old lady raised both hands and shouted — "shocking! horrible!" and called her friends to come and see such a wonderful sight, so that we had quite a group of market-women around us. Then papa told them we lived in a country where tomatoes grew, and that we enjoyed them in any way, either raw or cooked. This is n't exactly telling you about Dresden, but perhaps you will like to hear sometimes about something beside the houses and the people.

We are going to Saxon Switzerland, to-morrow, if it is pleasant; and then I shall have to walk a long way after we leave the cars.

Papa wants mamma to go to a concert, so I must go to bed. Perhaps I shall dream you and I are eating tomatoes together!

Forty-Fifth Letter.

DRESDEN.

Dear Susie:

Yesterday morning I had to get up very early, and eat an earlier breakfast than usual for we were going in the early train to the Saxon Switzerland, and it started about the time that we usually take breakfast. We were afraid it was going to be a rainy day, but the hotel people said the sun would come out and we should have a fine prospect. As we were going to the station we all thought that the part of Dresden near it, looked like Edinburgh, for the streets were broad and the blocks of houses very fine.

We had a nice ride, and it was just long enough to be pleasant, but not so long as to make me tired. There was one German man in the carriage with us who didn't know what language we were speaking, and he wanted to know what country we lived in. When papa told him we were Americans, he had a great deal to say about America, and a number of funny questions to ask; he seemed to think that the country must be small enough for us to know anybody who lived there, and he really looked disappointed because papa could not tell him about some of his neighbors who had gone there.

We left the train at a little station close to the river Elbe, (that is the river that Dresden is on,) and then crossed over to the opposite side in a boat. There were several people besides us, but we supposed they spoke only German, and it sounded very pleasant when a gentleman offered mamma a seat and spoke in English. The German here in Dresden is said to be a little different from other parts of Germany; the people sing their words, but we have not noticed it. When we left the boat we walked first through a village where boys crowded around us, begging to be our guides; and though papa told them he had been there before and knew the way, one little fellow followed us until papa had to give him a piece of money, and then he went back to wait for somebody else. Papa gave him some advice in English, just for sport, but I am afraid it would n't do him much good.

So we went on and on; papa cut a stout walking-stick for me, and we walked on mile after mile. The sun was shining, but we were more and more shut in by great rocks all around us, and some of them were immensely high, and looked as though they would fall upon our very heads. Trees grew on some of them to the very top. Our little path kept leading us on, and we came to some guide-boards; one pointed the way directly to the Bastei, and the other kept on in the valley to some strange places in the rocks. We took this one first, and after a while we came to a great cave made by immense rocks resting on each other, and afterwards to a narrow passage under rocks. Great rocks had fallen and lodged on others, and we crept under them, but I didn't like it much. We found a little house in the woods, where a man and woman lived. He was chopping wood, and she was washing clothes. In front of the little hut was a table covered with things to sell, such as photographs of the Bastei and little pictures made in the form of roses (I had one of those), and glass vases, and little wooden boxes full of moss. Mamma allowed me to buy one of these boxes, and we filled it with heather which we picked on the sides of the road. Because after we got back to the guide-boards again, we took the way to the Bastei, and the path changed into a road.

I was very tired before we reached the top, and yet we rested two or three times; but we were going up hill all the way, and it was hard. When we were almost at the top we saw a very high tower, and I wanted to go to the top of it; but papa said we should be tired enough without it. Very soon after there were some buildings where people lived, and in one was beer and refreshment for strangers. We were glad enough to get something to eat, for it was noon, and papa called for cold meat and white bread and butter. They brought us some nice cold venison, but had nothing but the black bread; for, as it had looked like a rainy day, they had not sent down into the valley for any white bread. But we were so hungry we enjoyed anything.

Oh, Susie, I wish I could tell you what we saw when we went out on the very edge of the Bastei! It seemed as though there was a great ocean of rocks all around us, and they were so high they seemed like the great cathedrals I had seen. Sometimes great trees were growing on them. Just below us, but still six hundred feet below, was the river, and the little villages, and a good way off was what papa said was one of the strongest fortresses in Europe; just think, made of these great rocks. It was fearful to look down from where we were; it made me dizzy, although there was a strong iron railing around us. And we were on the top of one of these high rocks ourselves! The highest one is called the Bastei. We went over the strong stone bridge which is built across some of the rocks, but it is almost awful to walk across it. Mamma was afraid for me every minute when I did not hold her hand, for all the places were so dangerous. We went down a different way from the one we went up, and through the oddest little village, hid away out of sight in the valley at the foot of the Bastei. We had a good ride back to Dresden; but I was so tired, I did n't enjoy it so well, but the day itself was about the best I have yet had. Would n't you think it would be?

FORTY-SIXTH LETTER.

BERLIN.

DEAR SUSIE:

The ride from Dresden to Berlin did not seem as long as I thought it would, because we stopped over night on the way at Juterbog. If you thought we had a funny time when we spent a night at a village inn, in the summer, you would have said there was as much to laugh at about our visit to Juterbog. If we hadn't left the cars at all, we should have reached Berlin about nine o'clock in the evening, and it would have been almost better if we had kept on; but papa had a feeling that mamma would like to see some curiosity there was in that little place, and he thought, too, that a hotel was very near the station. When we found how the case stood, we thought his first visit there could not have left much impression upon him; certainly the long distance hadn't.

As soon as we stepped out of the station house, we saw it was already very dark. We had been riding since three o'clock. Papa said he remembered we must go through an avenue of trees, and then he believed we should come to the village; but he was a little mistaken. We each took something in our hands,—I had the luncheon basket,—and we trudged on and on, until even papa was, I think, a little tired, though he only said that strange places seem longer to reach when it is dark. Almost all of the way we walked by ourselves, though sometimes German boys would come along, singing a song or whistling. When we reached the village we supposed of course we were nearly at the inn; but papa was again mistaken, for we walked through one very long street, and then another, and still another. It wasn't much such a walk as it is to walk down Washington street in Boston, in the evening, I can tell you. At first the houses were very small, and only one story high; but in the second street they were better. The streets were paved with little round stones that hurt my feet at every step. There were not many people in the streets. Sometimes we would meet a man to inquire the way of, or a dog would bark at us. We passed one house where we could see into the rooms, because there were no curtains, and we saw rooms full of men and women drinking beer. After we had passed a very tall tower, papa began to inquire of people for the Black Bear, which was the name of the inn. At last we were directed to a house, which certainly did not look neat nor pleasant, and the rooms were full of soldiers, smoking and drinking. But mamma and I were afraid to go in, and that wasn't the Black Bear, either; it was another inn. So we had to inquire again, and a woman led us to the very door. We went into a long entry, and papa opened a door on one side; but it was full of men, so he opened a door on the other side, and there we found a very comfortable room. A man sat by the table, but he said nothing but "Good evening." Papa said, "Can we spend the night here, and have a good room?" He said "Yes," and then he went out and sent in a servant-girl. Oh, how she gazed at us! She of course knew we were foreigners, though she didn't hear us speak English, because papa had told us to talk together in German, if we could. Papa said to her "bring us the best supper you can, and then give us nice beds." Pretty soon she came in with supper; what do you think it was? Some brown bread, cut in thin slices, with cheese between them, and beer. That was all we could have; but although we never had liked the black bread as it is called, we all ate a good deal of it.

Then the girl lighted a tallow candle and led us through the long entry, and up some stairs which were not painted but covered with white sand. As we passed the kitchen door, all the people of the house, I should think, put their heads out to see us. We had really a nice, clean, large room, though there were no curtains to the windows. After I was put in between the feather beds, papa and mamma left the light burning, (that was because I was in a strange house and me awake,) and went out in the street again to see something in an old church there. I did n't see it; but it was a very old chest that a man, named Tetzel, used to put money in. He lived when Martin Luther did, and was a very wicked man; he used to tell people he would pardon all their sins if they would pay him money. But when he had got a great deal, it was taken away from him, and the chest he kept it in has always been in a church in Juterbog. I did n't know when papa and mamma came back, and I did n't know anything till morning. We had a better breakfast than we had supper, and had time afterwards to get to the train in season, and then we came here to Berlin. I do n't know whether I shall like this city or not; we live in a hotel now.

Forty-Seventh Letter.

BERLIN.

Dear Cousin Susie:

I have been almost homesick since we came here, and wished we were back in our home in America again, for we have had such a time looking for rooms. I always like to go out with papa and mamma when I can in the day-time, and so for two or three days I have been with them a good deal, and—oh, how many flights of stairs I have been up and down! Papa has been trying to find a home for us near the Unter den Linden; that is the name of the finest street in the city, and if anybody can live very near it, then there will be only a little way to walk to a great many nice places.

It seems like being in a great city again to walk through the streets here; and I think it is a very handsome city, for I have seen some very fine looking buildings with statues on them, and there are splendid shops here, too; but you would think, Susie, just as I do, that it does n't seem much like any place we know in America. The sidewalks are so different, and the houses all seem to look alike, for they are all of pretty much the same color, and that is a light yellow or straw-color; papa says they are made of brick, and then covered with a sort of colored plaster; and then, besides,— but I forgot what I was writing about when I commenced this letter; you see I write just as I suppose I should talk if I was with you, only I can't know what you would say. I wish I could!

I should think the Berlin people all lived up stairs, for the lower part of the houses is full of shops, and the upper stories are where the people live. And papa says this is the general custom here, although in the new, fine streets there are no shops in the houses. The houses must be very large here, or else so many families couldn't live in one; for they seem to be full from the top to the bottom, and each family live in one story, so that they can't have some rooms up stairs and some down as your mother does, but all must be joined together. We saw all kinds of rooms and all kinds of people when we were inquiring for rooms. When any people have rooms to let, they hang a painted notice by the great street-door, and as we were walking along, if we saw one of these large cards at a good looking place, we would go up stairs till we found the woman who had rooms to let. Sometimes she would live in the first story (that is considered the best), and sometimes in the second, and sometimes we went up to the very top of the house, and then only one room, or two little ones, or we would have to walk through the bed-room — and perhaps that would be dark — to get to the sitting-room.

Papa and mamma didn't find any place that exactly

suited them, although two nice ones were promised the first of next month; so we came to this side of the Linden, in the same street where papa used to live when he was here before. I do n't like it very much; but it is n't so much matter to me after all, for when I am in the house I have my playthings and my books, and then I shall walk every day with mamma, and perhaps bye and bye I may go to another Kindergarten. My drawer that mamma has given me is just full of my playthings. I have to keep my box of blocks on the floor. Did I ever tell you, Susie, that I had them for a present one time when I was sick in Gotha, and could not go out for several days? They are one of the toys that I was promised I should have when we got to Germany, and of course they came. Every time I go out on the street, I see so many pretty toys I would like, and mamma says she sees beautiful pictures she would like, and I suppose papa wants something, too. Whenever I say, "Oh, dear, I wish I had such a thing!" papa always says,

"Man never is, but always to be blest."

He has to say it so often to me that I know it by heart; and by this time I understand pretty well what it means, though at first I supposed it was some of his fun.

But I should think I had written enough! I wish you would write to me as often as I do to you. Do you ever play with your wax dolly now-a-days? The German name for doll is puppe; is n't it funny?

Forty-Eighth Letter.

BERLIN.

Dear Susie:

I begin to like Berlin pretty well. Every day I take a long walk, but the streets all seem to look pretty much alike, except the Unter den Linden. That name means in English "under the Limes," but we always say the Linden when we speak of it. It is such a splendid street, Susie,— a mile long; and it is so broad that there are two or three places for carriages and one for horseback-riders, and two side walks, and one broad walk in the very middle under the trees. At one end of it is a very large stone gate; papa says it is one of the handsomest in the world,— certainly I can't think how one could be finer; and when any one stands by that, he can see down between the trees a whole mile to a great statue. Do n't you remember hearing my papa tell once about Frederick the Great's statue that he had seen in Berlin? how beautiful it was, and he hoped that when you and I were young ladies, we should see it too? Well, this is the same one, and I do n't wonder now that papa and everybody else praises it so much.

There is so much to be seen on this street, that if I should try to tell you what I see and how much I like to look at the splendid shops, you would say I was silly, and I am afraid cousin Mary and aunt Susan would think I should make you discontented. The king's palace is close to the great statue, and there are a great many fine buildings beyond that, and all have statues on them. When we get back to America I think we shall miss the statues some. Papa told me yesterday what all these buildings were: some are palaces, and the Crown Prince lives in the handsomest one. You know, do n't you, that he married Queen Victoria's oldest daughter, and I think she ought to have a pretty home here, when she had to leave such nice places in England.

But I began to tell you what was in these great houses. One is an arsenal, and is full of guns and swords; and another is where the great museum is, where I suppose there is almost everything to be seen. And opposite that, across the great square, is the old palace. It is so large that I should think a little city full of people could live in it. We went into it yesterday. Some more Americans went with us, and we had to have a guide. Did I ever tell you, Susie, about a young American gentleman that we used to know when we were in Bonn and Heidelberg? He used to make me think of your uncle Tenny and of my uncle Will, and I loved him very much. He is visiting us now, and went over the great palace with us. Of course we did n't see half nor a quarter of all the rooms; but what we did see were most splendid. The floors were polished so much that I could hardly walk without slipping down, and all the gentlemen had to put on soft sandals over their boots, to prevent any scratching on the floors.

Some rooms were full of portraits, and some of carving, and some of beautiful silver things. Oh, I was really tired seeing so much! and we kept walking on, from one great room to another, till we came to a church. It is made as a dome, and is round. Papa told me about all the kings and distinguished people who had lived in this palace, and we are going out to a pretty place some nice day, where there is another; but I suppose it is n't as splendid as this one.

I like to walk in the Thiergarten, and I take my great ball there to play. It seems like a great wood, only it has nice paths for people who walk, and carriage roads for carriages; and there are little ponds in it, and beautiful statues. There are always a great many people to be seen there, and papa says that in warm weather and on Sundays, it is crowded with people. We only have to go through that great gate I told you about, and then cross a street, and we are just on the edge of this Thiergarten; but it is three miles long.

I hope I shall write letters from Berlin that you will like, Susie!

Forty-Ninth Letter.

BERLIN.

Dear Susie:

The reason I have not written for so long is, because I have been so busy. I have commenced going to another Kindergarten, and I like it very much. That takes all my time, from nine o'clock till one, and then after dinner I take a walk, or sew, or read. Two or three times lately, mamma has taken me with her when she has gone shopping. I always want to laugh, because the shop women are so polite, and mamma makes such funny mistakes in German. I have just had a new hat; but we had to go into a great many shops before we could find what suited us. Oh, Susie, they think it is so funny in the Kindergarten, that I don't wear ear-rings in my ears, for the little German girls do!

I wish I could think of all I have done that you would like to hear about. I remember that we went out to see the palace in Charlottenburg, and we rode in the horse cars. It was so nice to ride in the horse cars again, for we hadn't seen any since we were in

New York; and I shut my eyes and tried to imagine we were at home again. The cars here are better than ours at home, because there are narrow stairs at each end for people to go up to the top and find nice seats.

The only thing I saw in the palace that I cared much about, was an old clock that used to belong to Frederick the Great, and could be wound up to play a tune. The music was so loud that I was almost frightened, and I don't wonder it made Napoleon jump when he heard it in the night. When he had gained a victory once, he came to this palace to sleep one night; and after he had gone to bed, some roguish servant placed this old clock beside him, and touched the spring. It began to play the old Prussian march, and it woke Napoleon up. He thought the Prussian soldiers must be coming upon him, and called for help.

There are two beautiful monuments of Queen Louisa and her husband in the garden of the palace, and strangers are all the time going to see them.

It is almost Thanksgiving time, and I really wish I could be with you on that day. I suppose you will have roast turkey, and mince pie, and plum pudding, for dinner. I don't think I shall see any turkey, for papa and mamma are going to eat their dinner with a great party of Americans at a hotel, and little children are not allowed to go. Every two weeks there are American gatherings at the ambassador's, or somewhere else, but I can't go there, either.

I know a few little girls here besides the ones in

the Kindergarten. Oh, we do have such nice times in my school! One day we make pretty things out of paper, another day we make nice things with worsted, and another day we prick the prettiest little baskets and flowers and vines in patterns with pins, and on Saturdays we always work in clay, and make anything we like. And then every day we have nice stories told us in German, and play amusing games besides. We do not sit still a great while at a time, for the teachers always have some plays ready. All the children, and the teachers, too, carry their breakfasts to school, and so mamma allows me to carry something in my little basket, though I have breakfast at home first. Some of the children carry brown bread and slices of meat, and some bread and butter; and the teacher has a glass of beer sent in to her. This is the teacher who lives in the house where the school is: the others don't live there. We all love her dearly, and she seems to love us, though she has taught a Kindergarten for a great many years. She and the other teachers are showing us now how to make pretty presents for Christmas. You see, Susie, every family here in Germany have a Christmas tree, and our school is going to have one, too; and we shall each have a little present, and take something off the tree for our parents. I am making a watch-case for papa, in the form of a slipper. It is made of brown pasteboard, embroidered with worsted. He doesn't know it, though, and I am going to try and keep a secret this time. Please, Susie, ask your mother not to write it to him.

I don't believe I can write any more letters till after Christmas, for I shall be so busy. I am going to have a little tree at home besides. When I can, I'll tell you about it all.

www.ingramcontent.com/pod-product-compliance
Lightning Source LLC
Chambersburg PA
CBHW020241170426
43202CB00008B/182